The*Lemurian* Way

Remembering Your Essential Nature

The *Lemurian* Way

Remembering Your Essential Nature

Lauren O. Thyme
with Sareya Orion

Lauren O. Thyme Publishing
Santa Fe, New Mexico
2017

THE LEMURIAN WAY: Remembering Your Essential Nature

For information contact:

Lauren O. Thyme Publishing

Thyme.lauren@gmail.com

LaurenOThymecreations.com
https://thymelauren.wixsite.com/thymely-one

Jacket/cover photo

dreamstime_xxl_83008949 creativecommonsstockphotos

Interior and cover design Sue Stein

Other books by Lauren O. Thyme:

Thymely Tales, Transformational Fairy Tales for Adults and Children, 2nd edition

Alternatives for Everyone: A Guide to Non-Traditional Health Care, 2nd edition

Forgiveness equals Fortune (co-authored with Liah Holtzman), 2nd edition

Along the Nile, 2nd edition

From the Depths of Thyme

Strangers in Paradise

Cosmic Grandma Wisdom

Twin Souls, A Karmic Love Story

Traveling on the River of Time, handbook for exploring past lives

Catherine, Karma, and Complex PTSD (coming 2018)

Special thanks to Sue Stein and Roy Briggs
for their hard work in helping make this book a reality.

What Others are Saying About The Lemurian Way

The Lemurian Way could be used as a guidebook for the new millennium!
—Alex Lumen, former art director, *Fate* magazine

Some of your book's concepts reminded me of Einstein's theory of relativity. I got out my *Relativity Made Simple* and found interesting correlations.
—Phil Stone, engineer and architect, Seattle, Washington

I really liked the book information on the Lemurian community bringing up the children. It really resonated. The whole book is great in that it is info about how people were like, which is information that is really hard to come by. And after all, isn't that really what we are all curious about, anyway?
—Andrew Lutts, Salem, Massachusetts, Salem Center Electronic Newsletter and Lemurian Mailing List Website

Fantastic! Wonderful! Soul Elevating! Thank you so much for your marvelous spiritual book. I thoroughly enjoyed it and I know I am a better, more whole person, because of you and this book. Those Lemurians really had the knowledge of how to live in the peaceful awareness of God's Grace! And they "just knew." So they were Love and Joy! I'm so glad you were born to write this wonderful book which can be read by all those souls who are ready for it! It's so special!
—Bernice Coffelt, Las Vegas, Nevada

Your book on Lemuria is fabulous and my mind began to flood with memory as I read each page. I could hear the voices of the Elders speaking. I wish you much success for there is tremendous power and hope in the words.
—Robbyne LaPlant, Owner/operator of Spiritual Journeys Sacred Tours, San Clemente, California

I started reading your book tonight...I am taking it slowly...allowing things to sink in...and several times I wanted to cry... the words just seem to reach deep

within, drawing out a feeling of Joy that has been dormant for so long…and flooding me with the feeling that I am truly and wonderfully LOVED. And I needed that feeling real badly tonight. What a wonderful book it is, Lauren.
—Robin Janice Burdick, Eugene, Oregon

I love your book *The Lemurian Way: Remembering Your Essential Nature.* This way of life feels so normal, so natural, so in balance with nature. It is hard to believe that such a perfect society would vanish. But it is not lost. We will bring it back-it is still alive in us. I have not yet finished your book, but so far I have not yet fully conscious recall on any of my Lemurian lifetimes, just feelings-a kind of attunement with that life style. It also explains to me why I have certain attractions, desires, or dislikes for particular things in this life time. Thank you for writing this book.
—Uschi Ursula Joy, Arlington, Washington

I really enjoyed reading your book. I've known for many years that I had life experience in Lemuria but reading your book made me feel like I was right back there. I was struck by how much that I want to tell you I read the book and it touched me in a very special way. I read it slowly and carefully. If I found my mind being distracted I stopped and refocused. It's a simple message but it is packed with powerful insight and has the ability to reach into the heart and raise it up. On two occasions tears came to my eyes. I read the last chapter at about 3:30 A.M. this morning when the world was still and quiet. I was taken into an alpha state where I experienced what I can only describe as "Spirit Sharing" or "Spirit Merging." Called into a meditative trance I began to a type of intent for increased understanding and awareness between family members and friends. I could see the violet light from my crown chakra and completed this prayer feeling emotionally and spiritually nourished and refreshed. Later this morning the Light phenomenon occurred again in the house, James [my husband] was aware of it too. It was the book that inspired the beautiful experience this morning. You have a very special and powerful gift.
—Sandra Randel, Astro-cartographer, Laguna Niguel, California

I finished *The Lemurian Way* last night. This morning I woke up singing for the first time in a long time and have been singing all day long!
—Demetria Daniels, free-lance writer, New York City

After 45 years in this "work" one quickly learns to discern the authentic from the inauthentic, and your magnificent Lemurian Way is so clearly a gift from Spirit directly to the life stream, which we are all a part!
—Ronald S. Ross, Stamford, Connecticut

Lemurian experience influenced me when I compared your description of Lemurian society with the way I have envisioned life in my community.
—Wm Uriel Andros, Fairgrove, MO, Order of Melchizedek

I received *The Lemurian Way* on Monday. It is wonderful. The memories are flooding in. I have stopped at the part about the Atlanteans embedding crystals in Lemurians' bodies and I will just sit with it until I remember. Do you remember me writing about the crystal in my third eye? Thanks for the book, it is a fabulous experience.
—Lilian Perth, Australia

After reading your book, I was "told" to go to my bedroom to sit and receive. During an hour and a half I was integrated with "my second half," which I described in my previous letter. It was very powerful! I was completely filled with high energy, and it became very hot. I used to work with high energies, infuse water and massage oils with the Masters and angels' energies, etc., but this was different. When the session was over, I realized that I and my "better half" had been joined into ONE. I tried after this to code some water with the Golden Light, and another with Kuthumi energy, and I must say that my energy power had increased many, many times! Now my body has to get used to these new, high energies before the next step. I know now that it's only a matter of days before a new reality will begin for me ... merging is happening since reading the book, but I knew the part with Kuthumi before that.. . the things concerning the Golden Light made a lot of sense to me. Thank you for

letting me share this with you!
—Ole Gabrielsen, Jutland, Denmark

I recently came across your book *The Lemurian Way* and read it with great interest. Then I googled your name and found your blogs. All very interesting. We seem to have a common interest and connection with the goddess Sekhmet among other things. I hope you are well and I bless you my friend!
—Maj-Britt Capener, Sweden

I have gone through the books on your Amazon page. I must confess you're such a gifted writer and I feel so honored to have crossed your path. Having to work for you is a treasure I'm gonna cherish for eternity. Thanks for the awakening your book gave me.
—Roy Briggs, Nigeria (re-typed the entire manuscript for the 2nd edition of *The Lemurian Way*)

In 2004 my book was translated into Turkish and published in Turkey by Akasa Publishers:
The Lemurian Way is part of my bedside altar.
—Akn Shn Ahu (Istanbul, Turkey)

We appreciate you and thank you for your book. Love from awakened Lemurian Sisters. We are looking forward to 2nd edition.
 —Akn Shn Ahu, Hale E. Bozaci, & Gokcen Isiltas Gulenc, Istanbul, Turkey

You are loved so dearly in Turkey, Lauren. Your book marked a pivotal moment in my awakening, personally...You have changed my life and path a lot with *The Lemurian Way*. Thank you for your being and sharing. *The Lemurian Way* is my bedside book, dear author. Hugs from my little corner.
—Selin Mikaela Bolu, Istanbul, Turkey

Love your book.
—Yogini Praxis Sari, Turkey

Love your book.
—Nergis Oner, Turkey

Lots of love for your book.
—Gokce Yesibas, Turkey

We are Lemurian friends now.
—Gulcan Demirci, Turkey

The Lemurian Way by Lauren O. Thyme is a fascinating account of the Lemurian civilization and, more importantly, what it meant to be a Lemurian. The wondrous civilization of Lemuria, having existed many thousands of years ago, can be a difficult subject to grasp. Certainly, as time has passed, physical evidence is more difficult to find. And yet the interest in Lemuria is stronger now than ever.

Lauren O. Thyme, with the guidance of channeled information from the Lemurian Elders, has created a striking account of the customs, lifestyle, and harmonious community of people known as Lemurians. This information is almost impossible to find anywhere else, and Lauren has done a masterful job of showing what life was like during this ancient civilization. The Lemurian Way includes chapters with surprisingly detailed accounts and descriptions of growing up Lemurian, the Lemurian Light Temples, childbirth customs, Lemurian communities, Lemurian vocations, rites of passage, a typical day in Lemuria, and much more.

From what information we can surmise about Lemuria, it was not a perfect civilization. Not only that, but it is believed that Lemuria was surpassed by Atlantis in terms of scientific and technological achievement. So what was it that was so special about Lemuria?

Lemuria was a civilization which valued the community, the individual, and a peaceful coexistence in the world. Lemuria rose far above third dimensional issues of struggle and strife. It was a civilization like none before it or seen since here on Earth. Lemuria, also known as the motherland or Mu, evolved to be a supremely ascended and fully conscious civilization. In fact, Lemuria is believed to have achieved the highest level of civilization on Earth. *The Lemurian Way* helps us remember that greatness within ourselves.

If you feel drawn to Lemuria, or Mu, for whatever reason, and would like to learn more, *The Lemurian Way* provides you with a truly wonderful understanding and awareness of the Lemurian civilization, and the glory that Lemuria was. And by exploring, studying and remembering our distant past, we can better understand why we are here now.

—Andrew Lutts, Founder, Salem New Age Center and the Lemuria Mailing List

Table of Contents

Foreword

The Lemurian Way is a mythopoetic message in the tradition of W. B. Yeats'
Vision, and before that in the utterances of the ancient Bards inspired by the
Muses. "Inspired" means breathed into. The poet, therefore, is a relatively passive receptor or conduit through whom the words are uttered. The Muses are
the daughters of Mnesomne, Memory. In this connection the authors of The
Lemurian Way are listening to the memories of those voices who call themselves the Elders of Lemuria, of a place and time thousands of years ago now
miraculously awakened.

    The Lemurian Way is mythopoetic also in the tradition of William Blake,
who said that "what can be imagined is real." It is an important quality of the
mythopoetic also that the conduits project their absolute sense of the authen-
ticity of the experience. The narrator of Genesis II-III, for instance, establishes
his/her authority at the text's outset. Horner, likewise, conveys the narrator's
sense of omniscient eyewitness in his description of the Trojan War. The truth
of the experience is here also, reified by the conduits' personal recollections of
life in Lemuria elaborated by the Elders. In a real sense, they are Lemurians,
imbued with the fervor of awakened spirits. In contemporary Jungian terms,
they have dipped into the collective unconscious beyond the restricting and
censoring influence of the ego and almost dreamlike, emerged into a fully ren-
dered vision of a lost civilization. Lemuria shares many components of arche-
typal realms: Edenic, its members enjoy a harmonious tribal, preliterate
existence of remarkable tranquillity and innocence. Then its disruption by
representatives of the intellect and its ambitions, in the form of the Atlanteans,
parallels the seduction of Adam and Eve by the ego-dominant Adversary."

    Here, too, is the hidden ambiguity of the felix culpa, the fortunate fall, in

3

which "the perils to which the flesh is heir"—of consciousness and experience —are a worthy price to pay for humanity's growth. The Lemurian Elders sadly realize their earlier failure to attain the harmonious balance between spirit and body and now challenge us to take up the task. Thus it has always been in the most treasured memories of the race to regain the possibility of "resurrection in the flesh"—a spiritualized existence in the here and now.

Quite true, the Lemurian here and now, the idyllic millennia rolling by in a seamless, light-suffused present, ironically comments on our fallen existence. Simple communal tasks, the daily warmth of familiar faces, the rituals of group solidarity echo in our dreams of Eden or in motion picture fantasies of the South Seas. Their births are preciously spaced; ours profligately strewn. Their sex is sacred; ours mimes images of ecstasy. Yet the tone of the Lemurian Elders is not scolding or shrill in the manner of a Jeremiah foretelling doom should the message go unheeded. They speak out of their own sadness at a chance lost. Theirs is a loving concern for those now who have the opportunity to turn to the Light. And finally, their message, as the conduits tell us, is not new but rather a profound restatement of those spiritual and ethical precepts that resonate timelessly in the utterances of wisdom-Sayers everywhere. Sagely also, their call is to the Single One, to each of us as an "I," who in the full meeting of the "Thou" of another, meets also God.

—DR. PAUL OBLER

Author's Note: Paul Obler, Ph.D., was a published literary critic, Professor of Comparative Literature, a scholar of myths and archetypes in ancient civilizations, and a licensed Marriage, Family, and Child counselor. He was my partner for 23 years until his death in 2013.

Preface

A Special Love Story

Lauren O. Thyme and Sareya Orion have their own soul memories of Lemuria and created this book in partnership with Lemurian Elders. The Elders, many of whom may be Ascended Masters, are a loving and gentle group of souls who advise and teach human beings the essential nature of the universe from their perspective in the spirit world.

The Elders describe the harmonious life they experienced in Lemuria as a guidepost for human civilization today. They elaborate on the ease of Universal Laws and Wisdom as they lived it, knowledge as old as humanity. Pieces of knowledge have been explored extensively throughout time in myths, legends, archetypes, philosophy, world religions, and mystic thought. Information has issued forth from countless shamans, prophets, mystics, philosophers, poets, psychics, and recently by transpersonal psychologists, scientists, and physicists.

However, the Elders' intention is to complete our education: to present the entire body of knowledge, kept secret for ages, to prepare for the leap in planetary evolution. To accomplish that, they stimulate deep soul memories by presenting details of their society that encompass the order, logic, and harmony of the universe. They remind us to allow recognition, knowledge residing in individual souls, to just happen. They encourage us, not just to understand with our intellects, but to feel the wisdom in our bodies. Most

3

importantly, the Elders quietly remind us that Universal Laws and Wisdom were initiated and put into motion by a loving Creator Source, so that everyone can live one's essential nature of peace, harmony, love, and joy.

Introduction

Many decades ago, when I was five years old, I heard disembodied Voices. As time went on, communications from these Voices grew more frequent and articulate. Accompanying the Voices was a sweetness, an unconditional love that was tangible. During those decades, the Voices (or the Guys, as I came to affectionately call them) began teaching me. Spirituality 101, I suppose you could call these lessons. The Guys were gentle but resolute, coaxing and encouraging. They were supportive and nurturing when I was down, enthusiastic when I made breakthroughs. I received messages from them that were detailed and coherent and always accurate.

Then the Guys informed me they wanted me to write a book on Lemuria. Lemuria was one of my favorite subjects, and my most beloved memories were of that time and place.

However, I refused, since I was working on another project at the time. The Guys didn't give up. With synchronistic brilliance I was introduced to Sareya Orion by a mutual friend, Liah Holtzman. Liah and I had just finished our joint book project *Forgiveness equals Fortune*, now in its 2nd edition. Sareya and I became instant friends and we began sharing our memories of Lemuria. Sareya wanted to write a book on Lemuria. I offered to help her to do so. The rest is history. She moved in with me and we began this project.

My role in the writing of *The Lemurian Way* was storyteller, sometimes that of scribe and editor. Sareya's presence (since she had been a librarian in Lemuria) acted as a battery for me, to generate information, to clarify my memories, and to add her own precious ones. In time, I began to realize that the Guys were and are Lemurian Elders. Suddenly my whole life came into sharp focus, and with it the book's powerful messages.

In Lemuria, the Elders' job was never one of power and control. Their task was to hold the energy of love, spiritual wisdom, knowing everything was connected to everything, and that all beings had their place in the universal scheme of things. In that same vein, the Elders worked with us in unison. They were supportive, communicative, and clear, knowing that we were all important in this project. Thus this book is not channeled but remembered.

At no time did I think of the Elders as being in charge, but rather as kindly mentors and guides. Without Sareya and me, their messages would not have found a human voice. So we were partners with the Elders. Because the Elders prefer to have others' own wisdom guide them on their unique spiritual paths, the Elders asked that nothing in this book be directive or advising. No exercises to perform. No lists of do's and don'ts. Rather they requested us to encourage the reader's own innate wisdom to emerge when reading the words and feel the intent behind those words. "Keep it simple," They told me.

I wanted to retain the Elders' unified, loving, gentle Voice, and to that end I endeavored to write the way I felt them. Several messages came through verbatim and I include them as such. I asked the Elders if they wanted to include exercises or to expound in greater detail. They declined, saying they wanted the reader to simply "feel the energy of Lemuria in themselves."

The Lemurian Way has changed Sareya's and my life forever, for the better. This book has acted as an important piece of a cosmic puzzle for me, putting many vague and sometimes disparate spiritual ideas into understandable, eloquent, and cohesive substance. I am grateful to the Elders for their unwavering patience, love, and communication. I'm grateful to Sareya for being an important conduit and Library to assist in bringing this body of knowledge together. And I'm grateful to myself as well, to be able to hear the Elders, as well as to write and edit what I heard and what I remembered on my own. We were a team, with everyone playing their most perfect part.

After this book was finished, the Elders merged with me and announced I was now an Elder in training. I felt the joyful responsibility of an Elder— holding the energy and continuing to learn and practice Universal Wisdom, to grow and evolve in an ever-expansive spiral of becoming, to encourage and nurture others on their spiritual paths.

I honor the Elders, Sareya, and myself—and I honor you. I have come to learn that we each play an important part in cosmic evolution. You, the reader, are a wisdom-bearer. You are a team player. We are all on the same team.

I've often been asked if my memories are real, if Lemuria was real. Whose reality? From what perspective? The more I learn, the more I realize I don't know anything, except my body /mind wisdom as it emerges in each present moment. Perhaps the Elders were only my own voice, my own wisdom. Or maybe I tapped into archetypes of paradise in the collective consciousness. Possibly Lemuria is the future. I've decided that, in the final analysis, there is no reality with a capital R.

One thing I do know, however. Writing this book, then living and practicing the Lemurian Way, makes my life, my work, and my relationships with others more harmonious, blissful, and fun. For me, that's the ultimate reality.

With warm affection and joyful blessings.

Lauren O. Thyme

Chapter One

The Magical Land of Lemuria

We call ourselves Lemurian Elders; we lived in Lemuria as Elders long ago. After the dissolution of our physical bodies and civilization, many of us felt we had made important errors during our time on Earth. Consequently, we made a mutual decision, to return to Earth in the form of spirit guides and teachers, to help others learn and grow from our mistakes. We've continued to transmit our messages ceaselessly, in service to humankind. There are hundreds of us who've assembled to continue our work for this beautiful and struggling planet. Although we have different characteristics, we speak as one voice. Furthermore, we consider all human beings as Lemurians whether or not they lived in Lemuria.

Our beloved motherland of Lemuria existed at the dawn of human evolution. We were one of the first groups to be embodied in evolved physical form, coming to Earth as *Homo sapiens* were emerging as a species. We, and others who arrived elsewhere on the planet as well, knew that Earth was to be a testing ground, a laboratory for the universe. We had a physical body, with organs, glands, circulatory and nervous systems, and brains like you do today. Our appearance was also uniquely human, walking upright, with an opposing thumb and fingers. We procreated then as now. We possessed intelligence, creativity, and abilities fully recognizable to you living in the twenty-first century.

However, we in Lemuria made certain decisions very early in our civilization. We immediately experienced many difficulties while living in Earth bodies and we were determined to retain full control by coupling with the spirit world.

The spirit world, which we could access at will, was a blueprint for our civilization. This realm, where all souls come from, return to, and relate to as home base, operates in total harmony, mutual support, unconditional love, cooperation, peace, joy, and wisdom. This spirit world foundation is used as a point of reference, a jumping-off place for souls to explore other worlds, dimensions, and the physical universe. Furthermore, souls in the spirit world instinctively know who they are and what they need to learn in order to grow and evolve. Thus, we in Lemuria decided to remain fully attached to and conscious of our spirit selves.

How did we do that? In those early days, human beings were underdeveloped, loosely connected to physical matter and the planet Earth. Therefore, we could choose how we operated within those bodies; unfortunately, many modern human beings no longer have that choice. We chose a combination of factors, spirit bodies predominating, while physical bodies were secondary. We called our spirit bodies "light bodies," since they consisted mostly of light, vibration, and energy. A light body is an immense, vibrating aggregate of shimmering color, of which an aura is a mere remnant, which simultaneously surrounded us and was immersed within our human flesh. Since all manifestation in the universe consists of degrees of vibration and energy, we favored accelerated vibrations, higher energy and less density, while connecting ourselves firmly to Creator Source and Gold Light.

Creator Source is Divine Consciousness, existing of the highest vibration and energy that contains creative forces to a vast degree. Creator Source exists before, during, and after creation and is the source from which all manifestation originates. Creator Source has been called God, Allah, Jehovah, and many other names, but these names can't begin to describe the all-encompassing realm of this loving, vast, unending, intelligent energy and vibration.

All souls, indeed all physical and nonphysical manifestations, are part of Creator Source and will eventually merge again with Creator Source. Conscious life forms also participate in co-creation with the Source. The physical universe is only a small portion of the total universe, which is made up of other dimensions, realms, time and timelessness, and non-material manifestations. Creator Source put into motion all the laws of the universe which operate harmoniously and continuously. If this sounds confusing, don't be alarmed. Even in the spirit realm, many souls are unable to fully describe or comprehend the Source. While in that realm, however, souls can feel, sense, and perceive the Source's tremendous power and energy as a tangible force surrounding, nurturing, and empowering them. Gold Light is the emanation of, from, and connected to Creator Source, itself a creative, regenerative force. Like a ceaseless river Gold Light flows from the spirit world into the physical world, transmitting harmony and other heavenly attributes. Since Gold Light contains the vibration and power of creation, it is the strongest light of transformation in the physical universe. Gold Light, with its attachment to all manifestation, also yields awareness of higher realms, other universes and dimensions and Universal Wisdom.

White Light, used by wise people on your planet for countless ages, is a different form of light, intended primarily for protection and healing. Gold Light, on the other hand, is more encompassing, expansive, and transforming than White Light.

Because of our ability to stay connected with the spirit world and Creator Source while infused with Gold Light, we became distinct from the rest of the human experiment in progress on the planet. Consequently, we could travel to the spirit world, other dimensions, galaxies, and realms at will, while staying attached to our physical bodies. Throughout many millennia we only grew stronger in our knowledge and talents, as we practiced and developed them to an exalted degree. We were delighted with our capabilities and eagerly shared our vast knowledge with anyone who wanted to know. However, like you, we never conquered our fear of living fully in our bodies. We preferred our light bodies to physical ones. When we donned our physicality, it was like donning a heavy, sodden woolen overcoat or stepping into frigid, deeply-disturbing waters. Whenever we immersed ourselves for extended lengths of time into physical totality, we began to experience sickness, unpleasant emotions, and a feeling of separateness from each other, Gold Light, and Creator source. So we maintained our vibration on higher realms, much like being in a highly altered state or astral travel most of the time.

In fact, the *only* fear that existed in Lemuria was in *becoming too human!* We knew what the human condition could lead to and we avoided that state of being at all costs. This was our failing, because the aim of incarnating on Earth was to become fully human, with all the delight and despair that might entail, in order to grow, learn, and evolve, while learning to stay attached to divine consciousness. Although we tried to elevate the rest of humanity to our level of aptitude, we failed that also and eventually our civilization began to crumble.

Then, to our great sorrow and horror, the land mass that constituted Lemuria began to rupture and separate, due to vast forces erupting in the Earth's core. Earthquakes, tidal waves, and volcanic explosions ripped our land asunder. Yet even as our beloved continent was breaking apart, to disappear forever from the Earth, we sent forth loving messages to remind others of our mutual sacred heritage. Parts of Lemuria submerged as the Earth's crust shifted. Oceans filled in the gaping wound, and many of us died. All that remains above water today is called New Zealand, Australia, the Pacific Islands including Japan, and to the east encompassing the western region of mainland United States and Peru. Due to shifting tectonic plates, volcanic upheaval, Earthquake activity, tidal waves, and the passage of so many thousands of years, there is little archeological evidence of Lemuria today. Remnants of roads are still to be found on some Pacific Islands, starting and ending at water's edge. But our ideas, lifestyle, and knowledge survive around the globe, especially in indigenous cultures, in lands where some of us fled to avoid the impending disaster. We believe Native Americans, Aborigines, Maoris, Peruvian natives, Hawaiians, Tahitians, Samoans, Tibetans, among many others, are our descendants.

We want to tell you a story not unlike the myths retained in those cultures: There once was a land of Truth and Wisdom, when the Earth was light and innocent and loving.

An enchanted land where everyone was wealthy in spirit and beauty, and all things that truly mattered were of the Light. Where food was plentiful and available to everyone and all of our needs were cared for.

Where bodies were regenerated in Golden Light Temples of Healing and health flourished. Where people lived together in harmony and happiness, and experienced blissful peace.

Where everyone was family and children were looked on as gifts. Where we frolicked, played, and sang together as a matter of course in everyday life.

Where communication between us was Truthful, Loving, and Respectful. We looked into one another's eyes and saw our True Essence reflected.

Dolphins, animals and plants, crystals and stars, mountains and the sea were also family, and we closely communicated with them all. We danced for joy and created out of leisure, while our spirits were happy and content. We came into this world knowing our gifts and talents so our jobs were fun-filled and playful; an expression of our greatest joy. We recognized our essential place in the Universal scheme of life. But this is not a fairy tale. It is a deep knowing. In fact; some of this knowing exists inside you right now! We have been waiting for this memory to fully awaken in you.

You are all Lemurians—and our message is simple. There's nothing to do but feel, and know in your deepest heart the natural state of your being, that you're not forgotten. You're not alone or lost. You have each other, and to have each other is to know God, to know the universe, to know Universal Wisdom. What your souls cry out for, hunger for, struggle to understand is so simple. It is love. Love of yourself, love of others, love of nature, and love of the universe. You know that. There's nothing new we can tell you. Open your heart and feel it, feel us, feel yourself. Let go of the hurt and let in the joy. It's so easy. Just let go. You are surrounded with love, nurtured and cradled with the Gold Light of Love. Feel it rock you gently in its arms. You are home, in the deepest heart of the universe.

The colorful flight of a butterfly. That is you. You are a beautiful winged creature, and need to know how exquisite you are. The flight of the eagle, that is you too. You are strong, wise, all-seeing, soaring majestically above the planet, your home away from Home. Remember the kiss of rain on your head. The whisper of wind in your hair. The awe of the song of a nightingale. The softness of a kitten against your skin. The feeling, knowing other dimensions, other worlds in a cell, in your orgasms of life, the profundity of a stone beneath your feet. You and they are one.

You and God are one. There is no separation except in your fears, in your nightmares, that you have forgotten the way. But we spread the crystals at your feet and light the way. The way is bright with moonlight and stars and candles and the glow of love reflected in your eyes for each other.

The only difficulty lies in not trusting what you know, what you feel, and what you most care most about in the world. That's it! Right there! That thing that you came here to do, to share, to give to the world. The torch burns brighter every moment. You are poised on the precipice. Don't look down. Look up. The butterfly and the eagle will carry you on their wings. You are not a burden. You are light. They can fly and so can you. So must you. You are an important piece. Without you there is no flame. Without you the universe is diminished. Without you there is no universe.

You are one with us. We enfold you in our arms. We nurture your sweetest dreams. We cherish your uniqueness. We long for you to be together with us, together. Come home. Come home now!

The Sacred "Becoming" Ritual

When children were born in Lemuria, we performed the "Becoming" ritual, aligning and joining their souls to their bodies, to local and global communities, Universal Wisdom and Creator Source. This was our holiest ritual to welcome a new soul to our community. We present to you our Sacred Becoming Ritual in a guided meditation form below, to provide an opportunity for you link up with you truest and highest self, with others in your human community, your precious Earth, and the cosmos.

You may choose to experience this ritual now or save it for later. Whatever you decide, we take this opportunity to welcome you home! Go to a quiet space where you won't be disturbed for at least fifteen minutes. Make yourself comfortable. Loosen any tight clothing, remove your jewelry and shoes.

Close your eyes and take a deep breath. Relax into your body. Imagine that you are lying on a clearing of soft sweet grass with lush foliage all around.

Their bright green leaves shimmer in the sunlight. You can hear birds singing in the trees. The azure blue sky above you is awash with clouds like cotton candy. You feel warm, comforted, and embraced by nature.

Take another deep breath and let it out all the way. Sigh if you need to. Breathe deeply into your solar plexus and pull the breath up into your heart as an ocean of love. In the distance, you can hear the sounds of a waterfall, gurgling over rocks down to a clear pool at the bottom.

As you take another breath, the aroma of fragrant flowers tickles your nose. They smell sweet and familiar. You hear the sound of drums and flutes gently wafting in the breeze. You become aware that the sound is slowly approaching you. The music fills you with joy and recognition. It's your brothers and sisters coming to visit you. You clearly hear their sweet voices singing a melodious song, one that you had forgotten but now remember.

As you lie in the clearing, eyes closed, breathing calmly, you feel them approach softly and gently, quietly singing their song. They form a circle around you. One of the people places a beautifully faceted crystal on your solar plexus, then returns to the circle.

Encircling you, they begin a slow delicate whirling dance and you begin to feel lighter and happier than you've ever known. As they sing and dance around you, you notice that each body is filled with and surrounded by a dazzling but soft golden light. The light from each body extends to all of the others until you are surrounded by their warm golden glow.

A vortex of Golden Light Energy swirls, encircling you and your family with powerful sweetness. The top of your head vibrates and you sense a spiral of golden light enter your head from above. Your feet tingle, connecting you to the Earth. Each of your sacred centers—the top of your head, center of your forehead, throat, heart, solar plexus, lower abdomen, genitals, and base of your spine begin to vibrate, glow, and swirl like pinwheels of light.

The pinwheels swirl faster and glow brighter and you become even more aware of them in your body. You feel your body connected to the Earth beneath you and to the stars in the heavens above you. You sigh in contentment.

You feel the Golden Light of joy, harmony, and oneness bathe your glands and organs. Engulf your brain. Circulate in your blood. Fuse into your bones and flesh. Each individual cell glowing and vibrating with Gold Light. You feel all problems melt away in the warmth of the Gold Light. You feel the connection of the Golden Light above, your crystal light body, and those of your family, singing and dancing around you…the oneness of all. You sense your cellular structure transforming, becoming more of who you are. Becoming the person you've always known you were meant to be. Brighter, happier, content, and at peace. And you are filled with excitement, because now you are Home.

Chapter Two

Life in Lemuria:
Venus Is Our Mother

Countless thousands of years ago our civilization existed on a large continent in what today would be called the South Pacific. The continent on which we established our motherland has also been known as Mu or Mukalia, but we'll use the term Lemuria instead. Lemuria existed both before and concurrently with the civilization you know of as Atlantis. However, our civilization disappeared millennia before Atlantis itself was completely destroyed.

Our souls had migrated from other galaxies such as Andromeda, Sirius, and Orion as well as other dimensions, then to Venus in your solar system before coming to Earth. As you know, Venus is uninhabitable for human beings. So we lived there in strictly nonphysical, vaporous bodies, similar to jellyfish, floating in the hot oceans of liquid gases, as did most of the sentient life there. Since we were formed of gases, we were able to closely intermingle with each other, just as smoke can swirl around and through itself. Sometimes a number of us occupied the same form simultaneously. We were asexual creatures, able to reproduce new life from within our sensitively undulating bodies without assistance from any other of our kind. We possessed great intelligence and consciousness, and the many ages we lived on that planet were incredibly happy and harmonious. In some ways Venus was our most favorite destination.

At a certain point during our Venusian evolution we unanimously decided it was time to learn about physical existence, something we had not yet experienced. We chose to venture into a form of intelligent life recently emerging on the lovely blue-green planet third from the sun in the same solar system as Venus, your planet Earth. We intuitively scanned the planet to find a piece of real estate that would be compatible to us and decided on the peaceful continent we call Lemuria.

Part of our attraction was the many water sources flowing in and around this area and intelligent sea creatures swimming in the seas that had also evolved from Sirius. Two vast oceans surrounded our country to the east and west. Hot springs, waterfalls, streams, rivers, and other water sources flowed plentifully. We settled our communities near fresh-running water, since water was both necessary for life as well as considered highly sacred. We knew that water, the lifeblood of Mother Earth, was a conductor of spiritual energy. Those of us who chose to live near the oceans established close connections to dolphins and whales. The Lemurians who lived inland developed a great affinity to waterfalls, streams, and forests.

Our land was mountainous in places, and we experienced intense volcanic and seismic activity at various times. The climate in our homeland was subtropical in the north and tropical in southern areas. Thus, abundant and lush vegetation flourished and our land teemed with an astonishing variety of animal life.

Venus' life force energy is harmonious and peaceful, and so was this beautiful continent we came to occupy. The vibration of our continent and people tended towards gentleness and peaceful coexistence, what you might call unconditional love. Although Earth was our first experience in human, physical form, we retained our Venusian ways with relish. Lemurian energy, therefore, was oriented towards harmonious relationships, cooperation, and peaceful group activity.

Through our long evolution we maintained a connection to Creator Source, Universal Laws, and Wisdom, and a supportive, interlinking collective consciousness which we brought with us. We were content and peaceful, but also joyful and fun loving. We realized that we had come to Earth, not only to learn to be physically human, but also to share our bountiful knowledge of wisdom, love, and respect for all Earth's inhabitants.

We the People

We Lemurians were tall and slender, with a handsome, pleasing appearance, dark complexion, dark eyes, and lustrous dark hair. We contained perfectly balanced male and female energy making us appear androgynous. Our Venusian energy inclined us, male and female alike, toward a feminine rather than masculine appearance. Although we had physical bodies, we didn't fully inhabit them at all times as you do today, but lived primarily in light bodies. These light bodies have been called spirit or etheric bodies, and were similar to our appearance in the spirit realm. The atoms and electrons were loosely spaced in these light bodies, giving us the appearance of being ephemeral and glowing with blue light. Our skin radiated a translucent, ethereal opalescence. We could access fourth, fifth, sixth, seventh dimensions, and higher. Thus we could change the vibration of our bodies at will, but without relinquishing our connection to physical form. The closest experience in modern time would be out-of-body travel or deep meditation, although significantly different, perhaps akin to the "Dreamworld," which some Pacific Islanders still preserve. We could detach and reattach our consciousness to our physical bodies, connected only by a cord of energy like an umbilicus. This energy cord was only severed at death. Although we were always attached to our bodies, we altered our consciousness and awareness for voyaging and learning in nonphysical or extraterrestrial circumstances. Each person was connected to and was a repository for the Gold Light, Universal Wisdom, each other, and the cosmos.

Grids, Energy Stations, and Light Temples

Our Lemurian civilization fluctuated between ten to sixty thousand persons at its zenith. Since we understood and utilized mathematics, cosmology (knowledge of the energies and vibrations of Sun, moon, planets, and stars), and sacred geometry, our communities were carefully designed and constructed on the planet as related to planets, stars, and galaxies. What was our purpose in using sacred geometry? Higher, spiritual vibrations resonate to specific geometric configurations.

Our continent was divided into the shape of a large six-pointed star, with a community hub based on each of the points. Extending out from and in direct alignment with each of those six hub communities we developed six other communities, also in the form of six-pointed stars.

The six-pointed star, two overlapping triangles pointing in opposite directions, had several meanings for us. The first incorporates the four elements of fire, earth, air, and water. The second represents physical consciousness striving to reach spiritual levels, while higher consciousness attempts to be effective and functional in the physical world. Thus, we used sacred geometric configurations to designate the four sacred elements found on planet Earth as well as higher and lower consciousness working together in harmony. The third, and perhaps most important component of the six-pointed star pertains to gateways. In our symbolism triangles represented beginnings and creativity. Two linked triangles (the six-pointed star) is a gateway, a portal through which one can travel in consciousness through time and other dimensions, where vital information and knowledge can be perceived and brought back into physical form.

The Earth body is like a human body with energy flowing through meridians known as ley lines. These ley lines are the Earth's nervous system. We called these ley lines grids. Our thirty-six communities were always placed on these grids, in accordance with and in relation to the sacred geometry of the land, the waters, other communities, and weather conditions. Our communities were linked along these grids to each other and the planet.

At certain points on these grids are "acupuncture points" that contain tremendous vortices of energy. We called these acupuncture points or vortices "energy stations." Like acupuncture is to the body, energy stations are connected to different points in the universe as well as to grids on the Earth. For example Glastonbury, England; Mount Shasta, California, and Lake Taupo, New Zealand, are all connected on the same Earth grid. Energy stations were and are virtual expressways of light and energy to other dimensions, planets, and galaxies, and the spirit plane, as well as to Earthly connections around the globe.

All interdimensional travel as well as to planets, stars, and galaxies was accomplished in consciousness only; we never took our bodies with us. We simply changed our vibratory levels and traveled in our etheric bodies, similar to out-of-body experiences.

We further enhanced the energy stations by creating Light Temples on them, placed in the center of each of our thirty-six communities. Light Temples were often constructed using pyramidal dimensions and configurations, although they were composed of primarily light and energy rather than solid structures. Our Light Temples were natural, without walls, and often without a roof, usually constructed of wooden poles connected to a foundation with a light cloth canopy overhead. However, our Venusian tendency towards beauty dictated that the foundation be created out of a mosaic of crystals and other sacred stones, the poles be highly polished and intricately carved with sacred symbols, and the cloth was finely and intricately woven and ornately decorated.

Energy stations were also essential for our existence, learning, and well-being. We used our Light Temples:

To maintain our connection to Creator Source and Golden Light

To heal, regenerate, and recreate our physical bodies

To permanently depart from our physical bodies (an alternative to what is currently known as death)

To travel in our Light Bodies around the planet

To travel in consciousness to planets, stars, and galaxies, and inter-dimensionally

To communicate telepathically

To accelerate our learning processes

Often these Light Temples were situated on mountaintops and under the ocean. Dolphins were in charge of the Temples underwater, known as dolphin chambers, and those of us who held the job of Elders were in charge of those on mountaintops.

Our Council of Elders traveled to Light Temples to commune and align with the cosmos, and held eminently significant meetings for the community. A Holy of Holies Light Temple was built on a sacred mountain in the center of the main six-pointed star in the center of our motherland. Elders from all communities would meet there, meditate, and resolve differences.

If we could travel in consciousness, why did we bother to travel throughout our Motherland? Each Light Temple contained different energetic connections, vibrations, purposes, and instructions to learn different lessons, and the energies of Temples had to be experienced in physical form. Therefore, we traveled physically throughout the continent to gatherings, meetings, celebrations, and rituals, particularly to attend birth and death rituals. Sometimes we chose mates from other communities at the ritual festivals. We brought gifts with us which we shared while visiting these other communities.

Although Lemuria was situated on a large continent, physical travel wasn't a problem. We had well-maintained roads aligned on the grids, paved with stone and crystals, which were interlinked to all our communities. In your modern conception of travel and time, these journeys might seem arduous and time-consuming, but we had all the time in the world, and amused ourselves by using our trips as walking meditations and group fun. The roads were interspersed with communities and Light Temples, at which we could rest and refresh ourselves with fellow Lemurians during a long journey across our land. Furthermore, grids followed Mother Earth's dynamic body, which strengthened and energized us. In addition to physical journeying, we could travel telepathically, psychically, and inter-dimensionally throughout our land.

Gold Light: Refreshment for the Soul

Our Light Temples became portals where Gold Light from Creator Source streamed to Earth most powerfully. Gold Light was our lifeline to our divinity. This Light is a homing beacon, directly received from and is the light of Creator Source and is the strongest light for transformation and transmutation on the physical plane. We were infused with and surrounded by this light, which helped us access Universal Laws and Wisdom, as well as connect us to nature and each other. Gold Light was strengthened by attending rituals in our Light Temples. Furthermore, we knew that every manifestation of Creator Source was created from Gold Light.

In the Beginning before Beginnings was the Void.
Out of the Void came the Light.
The Light was called Love and it was Good.
All things come from the Light, will return to the Light, and can bask in
the Light.
Light is Love, and Love is all-illuminating.
But let us start upon the path to knowing WE ARE THE LIGHT.
—*Lauren O. Thyme, 1972*

Gold Light from Creator Source was very powerful, sometimes feeling like a shower of light, a flowing river of vibration, a vortex or cyclone of swirling energy. Gold Light was able to remove pain, create, regenerate, and recreate our physical bodies, and connect us to each other in an indestructible link of energy. It could also refresh, harmonize, and evolve our light bodies.

Daily Life: Life Is a Celebration

Living in Lemuria was like living in the mythical Garden of Eden. Time seemed to slow down or even stand still. Cares and worries evaporated. The energy was conducive to languidly eating juicy, ripened fruits while relaxing in carefree bliss. "Hurry Up!" was never a phrase used in Lemuria. The tropical and subtropical foliage was abundant with fruits, vegetables, herbs, and berries ripe for the taking.

Each significant event was widely celebrated as sacred and enjoyable. We always had a reason to celebrate, to play, and to have fun. Fun was the order of the day. If an activity wasn't fun, we didn't do it. We knew that fun and Light contained a similar vibration, which made fun enjoyable as well as spiritually enriching. Our days were spent being creative, playful, and joyful.

We believed in non-ownership of everything we found on the planet, and joyfully shared what we created. Consequently possessiveness, jealousy, competition, envy, and pride was practically nonexistent. We loved making presents, and giving them away. We knew that giving and receiving was the same thing. The more one gave, the more one received. We experienced spiritual wealth and abundance beyond current-day comprehension. Each man and woman, in his or her own way, made beautiful objects for the joy of creative expression: beauty was another gift from our Venusian experiences. We didn't make many things, but what we did create was carefully made, exquisitely beautiful, and lavishly decorated.

Our love of beauty gave rise to myths about very ornate and elaborate housing, buildings, even massive cities supposedly created by us. These records are mistaken. The Atlanteans, who visited us late in our civilization and ultimately settled on our homeland, were the ones who created marvelous structures, merging our knowledge with their technology, which we'll discuss in a later chapter.

We had plentiful feasting, parties, and gatherings. We not only feasted on food, but on each other's enthusiasm, aliveness, and joy. We pampered each other with soothing applications of clay packs from the riverbeds and merrily finger painted sacred symbols on one another's body before the clay dried. We braided flowers and herbs into one another's hair, applied sacred essences, and massaged each other. We sang to each other and adorned ourselves and others with crystals and seashells. We dressed ourselves in flowing translucent cloths woven from the finest fibers and Gold Light.

We created magnificent cloth similar to tapa cloth used in Polynesia, but much softer and more intricate. We beat fibers of bark, leaves, and plant material, then wove the fibers into cloth. We utilized a special knowledge of weaving Light into our cloth, which made it delicate and airy, suitable for our warm climate. Then we decorated the cloth with sacred symbols and other designs using dyes from crushed plants, flowers, minerals, and rocks. This cloth was subsequently used for clothing, decorative applications, and bedding. We collected leaves, soft plant materials, flowers, and herbs to place under our bedclothes, which made our beds comfortable and pleasant smelling.

Our work was playful, fun, and interactive. We joyfully worked together and assisted each other with building homes. We kept our lifestyle uncomplicated, because we wanted to stay close to nature and to avoid any entrapments into physicality and all its attendant problems. Thus, our housing consisted of simple thatched huts, sometimes adding decorated clay bricks as a portico, but open to the fresh air and greenery around us. We lovingly decorated our homes with crystals, wind chimes, and flowers. Our homes were easy to re-build after storms had destroyed them. If we tired of one, we could easily build another.

We also collectively gathered food. There was plenty of food for all, which was freely nurtured, gathered, and shared. We didn't implement farming and agriculture, because we felt to do so was to upset the balance of nature and to interfere with the natural cycles and growth of plants. Therefore, we only har-vested the food growing wild all around us. We worked in harmony with the land so food was enormously abundant and nutritious. We blessed and loved the plants, visualizing and beaming light to the plants to fertilize and prevent disease. Insects were invited to share in the bounty, but the insect population generally took only a small percentage of our crops.

Our predominantly fruit and water diet nurtured and enhanced our light, multi-dimensional bodies. We also included vegetables, herbs, roots, tubers, nuts, seeds, and herbal drinks in our diet, especially a potent drink made from special beetles. These beetles were considered highly sacred and were used only for healing rituals and important celebrations. Our beetles were colored a bright, iridescent green and looked like small scarabs. Later on, the Egyptians would revere scarabs much the same way as we did. We stewed the beetles and ate them, then saved the broth to make an effective drink in order to activate higher vibrations while grounding our bodies with the Earth plane. We pre-ferred the aliveness of fresh food, though, so beetles were the only food we ever cooked.

Some of our community members created herbal and flower essence drinks, oils, and elixirs for healing and rejuvenation. Because we understood how to heal and regenerate the physical body, there was little pain, illness, or disease. Death was an event we could control and, when desired, will and in-tend to happen through transmutation and relinquishment of the body.

Everyone was a teacher for the young, according to their talents and pro-fessions, our best and most loved creative expression. Even prior to birth, souls had their own gifts, talents and personalities. Everyone's essence was apparent and we knew our gifts came from Creator Source. Power came from knowing and living our true essence.

Because there was no separation between our light bodies, there was no separation of thoughts, feelings, desires, emotions, or goals. Thus we possessed what could be called telepathy. With such a close and complete connection to each other, we lacked any need, desire, or ability to lie. There were no secrets. Subterfuge and deceptions couldn't exist.

Since we experienced no separation from Creation either, we could also read the cosmos. We naturally possessed psychic abilities you call precognition, clairvoyance, clairaudience, and clairsentience. Each person intuited Universal Wisdom and Universal Law and acted accordingly. We listened to our body's signals, trusted, and followed them. We rested when tired, ate when hungry, sang when we felt like singing, and so on.

We had no heroes. Everyone was equally capable and uniquely gifted. We were loving, knowledgeable, and dedicated to helping one another along the path of mastery in human form. We knew everyone was created by Creator Source which created the laws of the universe.

Creator Source was infused in all existence. When we touched another's hand, we knew we were touching the hand of God. When we gazed into another's face, we saw the face of God. When we trod gently on the Earth, we were walking on God's body. When we surrendered to life as we found it, we were snugly cuddled in God's lap.

Crystals

We highly revered inanimate manifestations of nature—mountains, oceans, rivers, streams, rocks, seashells, crystals—all played their essential parts in nature. Crystals were especially valuable to us. We found them inside caves, on the sides of mountains, in waterfalls and streambeds. Our general category of crystals included not only the many types of quartz and others crystals, but also what you call gemstones and semiprecious gems of every color and variation. We used crystals as energy conductors (transponders). Like a radio or radar set, we knew that crystals emitted signals, as well as responded to, transmitted, and amplified energy. So crystals were hung in trees, placed along footpaths, situated strategically in Light Temples, adorned our bodies, added to our homes, and used in all rituals. We also implemented crystals to regenerate our bodies. Because crystals were part of nature and energy, they were our companions. Although we used them as tools, crystals were seen as a willing, cooperative part of our community.

We not only adorned ourselves with crystals; we knew we were crystals. We contained a crystalline-like light body, through which we could send and receive information as well as to enhance certain energy fields and vibrations.

Love

Love was natural and effortless. We practiced loving one another in mutual respect, harmony, adoration, honor, and reverence for each other as well as for all life. Thus we kissed, cuddled, and stroked each other often out of our desire for oneness, exchange of energies, healing, and pure joy. Because we knew that each person was a sacred creation originating from the Source, our intimacies were holy and pure. Rather than touching one another out of sexual need, loneliness, emptiness, or a manipulation to gain love or security, our affections were viewed as a sacred sign of respect, unity, empowerment for both people, and unconditional love.

We practiced loving detachment and joyful connectedness simultaneously. We experienced what could be called "tribal consciousness" rather than being self-centered. Although we honored and respected each member's individual talents, abilities and gifts, we saw ourselves as part of a group, a vital and powerful collection of individuals.

Members of each community took turns living with one other, sometimes in couples or in larger groups we called families, quite unlike the modern Western concept of family. (We will describe this further in chapter 3.) These families consisted of all ages, genders and job descriptions. If we had a mate, we lived with our mate in holy union. Peace and happiness wafted through our homes as gently as the ocean breezes rustling nearby palm trees.

Nature and we were one, inseparable, made of the same stuff, part of the same cycle of life. We knew that sacred knowledge lived within plants, animals, and the cosmos, which instinctively knew when to procreate, live, and die. All that we found in our homeland were our friends—rocks, plants, streams, waterfalls, mountains, the sky, trees, the stars, the sun and moon and all animals.

We mutually communicated with and sought out friendship with animals on land and in the sea. Although some of these animals were fierce hunters, fear was not a word in our vocabulary. We communed with them out of love, camaraderie, and mutual respect. From them we learned their animal ways, sounds, and wisdom. Because we never hunted and killed them, animals found no reason to fear us, either. We didn't domesticate animals as is done today. We felt animals needed to live in their natural habitat, living the life that was part of their innate intelligence. Many animals became our friends and loved to be in our presence, often sleeping in our homes with us, joining in our rituals, and journeying with us as we traveled.

We weren't separate from these manifestations of Creator Source, but were one with them, and they with us. Because of that we felt at home everywhere, with everything. We could go into the dense forest alone or swim in the deep oceans and be unafraid. There were no enemies, nothing to fear, nothing to protect ourselves from.

We didn't enjoy being mean, because to hurt anything or anyone was to ultimately hurt ourselves. Only love, joy, and trust was represented in our communities, in a land full of unconditional love.

Sex

We changed homes and families often. We were also free to choose a mate or not, as we wished. As we have said before, we sometimes elected to live with a mate in sacred, holy union for long periods of time. Because of the lack of jealousy and possessiveness, we could change mates or be intimate with any person we cared to share ourselves with providing he or she was sexually mature. Although holy union with a mate was meaningful and life-enhancing, we might opt to have intimacy and/or sex with others. However, our activity generally wouldn't be considered sexual by modern terms and usually had very little to do with intercourse. Rather we joined together in our light and physical bodies for a mutual sensuous expression and interaction of partnered energies, harmonic vibrations, unity, enhancement of our physical and light bodies, and unconditional love.

When we did choose to enjoy full physical, sexual expression, our intentions and activities were also highly spiritual, akin to tantric sex. We utilized eye contact and breathing techniques, bathing, massage and gentle stroking, and rocking. We shifted our vibrations from higher realms and other dimensions into focused physical form, in order to experience sex fully in our bodies. Mutual orgasms were experienced physically, mentally, emotionally, and spiritually.

Atlanteans and other societies who visited us completely misunderstood our sexual practices. We were not at all promiscuous, although we may have appeared so to them. Intimacy was not engaged in lightly or trivially, but with definite spiritual intent and for the highest good of all concerned. No one "owned" anyone else, not even one's mate, so there was no reason to feel cheated. We knew that Creator Source had purposefully given sexual ability to humans, and we regarded sex in that light. Sex, therefore, was not considered taboo, dirty, unclean, immoral, but just the opposite—a sacred, holy, and special opportunity to merge with another in light, joy, and spiritual/physical ecstasy. Furthermore, no one in our society could be considered "sexually addicted" because addictions came from emotional pain, loneliness, and emptiness, which we lacked in our group consciousness.

Except for mating rituals, the purpose of our sexual activity was for fun, pleasure, and sacred communion with another and Creator Source, not to create babies. We practiced birth control with our minds, spirits, and energies. We also performed a Fire Dance ceremony, often aligned with seasonal changes. During Fire Dances, we lit bonfires and danced around them and ate special foods, including beetles and beetle broth. We sang, chanted, and toned sacred sounds, while our musicians played. The Fire Dance was intended to stimulate the kundalini and ignite all energy centers. One purpose of the Fire Dance was to activate our sexual feelings to a fever pitch, during which we reached extremely high states of spiritual/physical/emotional ecstasy. Often we would come together to experience intimacy with one another during this special time. Another purpose was to fully alter our bodies, becoming more physical. The third reason for this ceremony was to initiate our young men and women into full sexual activity, to teach them the spiritual / sexual skills and understanding needed as they matured. The Fire Dance was also employed during mating rituals. We viewed the physical body as a vehicle to experience life and pleasure, as well as to access higher wisdom.

Moon Times

We knew the value of solitude and took time out for ourselves, and communion with nature, when our bodies informed us of their needs. Full Moon time was always honored as a sacred time to be with oneself. During these few nights everyone become quiet and contemplative. The two weeks from full to new moon was considered a restful period, to meditate, contemplate, and integrate, and the pace of our villages slowed. All of us—men, women, and children—became exceptionally psychic and more receptive to Universal Wisdom. We meditated during the full moon, sitting quietly under its majestic orb, sending thanks to the Creator Source for the richness of our lives and the abundance of our planet.

All women menstruated simultaneously during the days of the full moon and they retreated joyfully to their moon temple. Our women were especially revered, considered holy and sacred. They looked forward to Moon Time to gather together in feminine unity, honoring the gift of creation, the Earth, and all its inhabitants. The women utilized this sacred gathering to strengthen their bonds of womanhood with each other, to view each as a consecrated vessel for Creator Source. Nurturing, love, creativity, receptivity, and other feminine attributes were honored and exalted. During Moon Time women spent many hours in close proximity, nurturing each other, meditating, and visualizing strong unity for their community. They also attended to weaving, pottery, and making art objects in blissful female union. Menstrual blood was sacred, powerful, and high in nutrients. So they spilt their blood on Mother Earth in and around the community compound, to bless, sanctify, and protect it. The women also mixed their blood with water to nurture and fertilize edible plants which would then more abundantly provide for their people.

The men also celebrated their masculinity and unified masculine energies. They cared for young children during the women's Moon Time and provided food for everyone. Men and children collected shells, crystals, and other ornamentation, carved and polished beautiful wooden objects, made decorative golden bowls of sacred beauty, and they all frolicked with each other in joyful playfulness and games. From the new to the full moon was a very productive time outwardly, and we performed most of our work during this phase of the moon.

The Elders—Sacred Keepers of the Light

Our Sacred Council of Elders were consulted when a decision affected a whole community. Although disagreement or dissension between individuals or communities was rare, when this occurred, the parties involved consulted the Council of Elders to attain clarity and regain harmony.

The Elders' inborn talents lay in the areas of accessing and holding Gold Light for the community, accessing Universal Wisdom, and supporting others. They held the energy for the collective vision and kept each other clear. Being an Elder meant using wisdom respectfully, and was not based on age. The Sacred Council consisted of men and women chosen before birth, their preordained gifts and talents accentuated by the configurations of sun, moon, planets, and stars, and appointed according to the needs of a community.

They were specially trained and apprenticed by current Elders in accessing and teaching Universal Laws and Wisdom, invoking Gold Light, understanding the vibrations of sun, moon, planets, and stars, protecting the bridge between dimensions and the cosmos, and supporting our communities.

While the Elders "held" the energy for us, they weren't considered more powerful nor given power over us. They simply had their job to do, acting as trustees for our society. Because the Elders accessed Universal Wisdom on a daily basis, people deferred to their abilities. Each Council of Elders made decisions for their community, and the thirty-six Councils for the collection of communities, in order to keep us connected to the Golden Light, Divine Guidance, and Universal Wisdom.

All their decisions were made with this intent in mind and were the closest thing to "law" that existed in Lemuria. Although our civilization and society appeared simple on the outside, everything was carefully considered and orchestrated down to the tiniest details. Mating, childbirth, child rearing, life's work, and continuing education were meticulously planned, although leisurely executed, and are discussed in the following chapters. The energy and timing had to be correct, based on information received in our group body from Creator Source. When energy and timing were favorable, we proceeded. Blissfully happy and harmonious in our relationships and our lifestyle, we lived peacefully and joyfully together for tens of thousands of years.

Chapter Three

Mating, Pregnancy, and Birth: It's a Family Affair

Since we lived to be hundreds or even thousands of years old, birth control was highly developed and collectively agreed upon as essential. We knew we had to keep the environment in balance, maintain a constant food supply, while focusing our undivided attention in training, educating, and continuing the evolution of our dear young ones.

To limit the number of births, we used a highly developed physical, mental, and spiritual procedure which simply blocked the sperm and egg from joining, to avoid producing new life:

Physical—Because we experienced sexual pleasure mostly while in our light bodies, the opportunity for an egg and sperm to join was practically nil.

Mental—We were meticulous in every way. Therefore, we had a back-up system of intention, a method of visualizing sperm dying and the egg passing through the woman's body into oblivion, to prevent conception.

Spiritual—We intuited when a new life could be possible. We withheld our sexuality at those times, to prevent premature pregnancies.

We scheduled births periodically:

- To promote new generational energy
- To promote growth and variety to our communities

- To stimulate and evolve our society with fresh talents, abilities, and personalities through varying individual components as aligned with planets and stars.

Thus a single birth might not occur for ten up to one hundred years. But when the time was ripe for the emergence of a new life, our entire community felt a yearning deep in our group consciousness. This was equally matched by the longing of many souls wanting to come into a physical body, explicitly a Lemurian body.

When a community intuited the coming birth of a new soul, the Council of Elders withdrew to their sacred temple of Golden Light, to meditate, connect with Creator Source, and converse with "souls in waiting." They summarized each of the souls' planetary influences, similar to using astrology today, considering not only influences from the sun, moon, and planets, but also galaxies and stars. Then they compared the souls for compatibility to the community. Even prior to incarnation, souls had their own gifts, talents, and personalities. Envisioning the highest evolution for everyone, the Elders reached a reciprocal decision.

Now the Elders and the "chosen one," as aligned with Creator Source, prepared to select the mother-to-be. They determined the compatibility of the planets and stars with each of the potential mothers-to-be and the soul in waiting. Of a community of hundreds of women, only a dozen or so were considered suitable. Age was not a requirement nor a consideration.

How did they determine the dozen women? They looked for the closest matches to the spirit of the soul-to-be and soul connections between potential mothers to child as well as their compatibility from other lifetimes.

Each woman was also assessed for:

- Strength to hold the Gold Light connection while maintaining a physical body,
- Beauty that radiated from her soul to love and nurture,
- Deep knowledge and practice of Universal Law and Wisdom.

The Council of Elders interviewed each potential woman with questions similar to the following:

1 **Are you willing to surrender your life to the honorary task of carrying a child for nine months?** A woman was totally free to decide whether or not she desired to become a mother. Although to give life was a great and rare honor, a woman might be involved in some important, creative work for the community and decline the honor.

2 **Are you willing to live in a more densely compressed and earthbound physical body for the period of mating and pregnancy?** We had discovered through trial and error that people had to assume a dense physical form in order to:

- Create sperm
- Have a man's physical penis enter a physical vagina
- Allow sperm to connect with a physical egg
- Permit a baby to grow within the mother's womb for nine months.

This difficult task of lowering our vibrations into solid physical form was uncomfortable compared to the lovemaking we experienced in our light bodies. Furthermore, once pregnant, a woman would have to continue to stay in this physical state throughout the nine months in order for the fetus to grow normally into a physical baby.

Lastly, a mother would be separated from the comfort, love, closeness, and security of the community in a way she had never experienced before. She would be physically secluded for the first six months of her pregnancy, isolated from the communal family.

3 **Are you willing to bear a child and then give it up to the community?** A woman was required to detach from the role as the baby's sole mother or caretaker at birth; a village communally parented a child born within its boundaries.

Our community began a grand celebration of feasting, singing, dancing, music making, and games that lasted for weeks. The thrill and delight of knowing a baby was coming and the wonder of who was to be chosen as the mother-to-be mounted as the days passed. The Council of Elders gathered in the sacred Temple of Light, meditating and fasting, while in constant contact with the new soul and Creator Source, to select a mother. They elected her jointly, unanimously, and unequivocally and joined the community's celebration.

At the pinnacle of excitement, the Elders announced the name of the new mother. As guest of honor, she was adorned with seashells, crystals, flowers, and herbs and given special foods as the feasting and celebrating continued.

Then the Council and the mother-to-be withdrew, fasting and meditating on the selection of the men to be included in the fertilization process. They considered each man in the village and carefully compiled a list of suitable men as potential sperm donors. This list might include as many as fifty men. The woman's mate (if she had one) might or might not be included on the list. Selected men might have had mates of their own. None of that mattered. Jealousy and possessiveness, as we have stated before, were nonexistent. In her absence a special house was built on the outskirts of our community and decorated to enshrine the mother-to-be. This home, open on all sides to the fresh air with a clear view of the greenery around it, was especially lovely and comfortable. Once it was completed, no one was allowed inside. Some artists spent days carving sacred symbols on the wooden posts of the house; others hung their favorite wind chimes in nearby trees. Crystal workers found the most beautiful crystals to adorn it. The Elders and healers, sitting outside on the ground, spent many hours chanting, visualizing, and intending Gold Light as well as the pink light of bliss in and around the house. Gardeners picked innumerable bouquets of the most fragrant flowers and set them in containers around the perimeter.

The Elders and the mother returned to the village when they had finished the perfect selections, to make their announcements. The elated "village-to-be" had continued celebrating and now the men selected were adorned, honored, massaged, stroked, groomed, and given special foods to eat. One of them would become the father of the glorious soul to be.

At that point the mother-to-be withdrew to her new home to prepare herself for mating. She altered her consciousness and began the process of submergence into physical form.

Everyone was involved in the courtship ritual. The community sent her

Gold Light, love, and support, in order for her to deal with her shift into physicality. Food and other needs were provided for the woman and her potential lovers. Villagers collected wood for the sacred fires to burn continuously. Musicians played their instruments, while singers sang and chanted, to provide a backdrop of sacred sound. The Elders, in a deep meditative trance, held a sacred space throughout the long ritual.

A tangible aura of lovemaking was created. Musicians and singers took turns playing music during the long days and nights, while campfires burned continuously. The villagers sang, chanted, meditated, and evoked the pink light of bliss around the entire compound. The selected men gathered in a special house of their own, on vacation from all activities. They were honored, given special foods and herbs to eat, massaged, groomed, and stroked, and generally taken care of by the rest of the community. They remained in a receptive state, holding the highest energy to bring to the woman.

The woman could easily connect with many men daily during this state of impending spiritual/ sexual union. Her body, mind, soul, and spirit were aligned with the essence of spiritual mating at all times until she conceived. The woman would intuitively know which man to call and when. She chose a man based on her timing and desire.

The woman prepared herself, her home, and her awareness for the ceremonial love making. Before the mating rituals began, she created the courtship bed. She gathered moss, soft grasses, sweet herbs, including lavender, aromatic flower petals like plumeria and ylang ylang and made them into a mattress, covered by soft cloth. She performed this creation by herself. Since touch was so potent, and so sacred, no one except the mother was allowed to touch it. Otherwise, other people's energy would be absorbed into the mating bed, creating confusion.

She sprinkled petals and herbs around the room and arranged sacred crystals in ritualistic patterns around the large room. Wind chimes made of wood, seashells, and crystals tinkled gently in the breeze. She remained in an intensely altered state throughout her courtship.

When called, a man went to the woman's new home to begin the mating ceremony. He brought love offerings such as crystals, cloth, shells, freshly picked berries or other fruit in highly polished wooden bowls, and beautiful decorative objects.

The couple performed honoring rites to each other and to the Source of all life. The mating ceremony started with a bathing ritual, since water was sacred. This was performed in nearby waterfalls, streams, or the ocean for communities near the sea. The ritual was performed, not only to wash each other's bodies, but to cleanse their light bodies of any impurities and attachments except to each other and the soul-in-waiting, while absorbing the divine essence contained in the water. In the distance, sounds of drums and other instruments could be heard, and the man and woman danced and frolicked playfully with each other in the water.

When they returned to the woman's home, they leisurely and gently massaged each other, using oils infused with flower, herbal, and crystal essences, as well as light energy. Their sexual energy increased, building a bond between them, electric but unhurried. Pink and gold light filled the room, swirling in ethereal bliss.

Then they adorned each other with flowers, shells, crystals, and shimmering, translucent golden cloth, woven by villagers trained in the art of etheric weaving and cloth making. They sat facing each other on the soft, fragrant mattress. Legs wrapped around each other. Gazing into each other's eyes. The woman knew when to begin the Sacred Breath, and they began to inhale and exhale in unison, while also breathing in the energy of the soul of the baby. Breath was a very important part of this ritual. Gold Light from the Source poured into the top of their heads, energizing and cleansing them at even deeper levels. Then golden energy began to pour out of the man's genitals into the woman's vagina, up through her body, out of her head, and back into the top of his head, down through his body, and back into hers, creating a continuous loop of energy connecting their bodies and energy centers. They breathed deeply and rhythmically and their bodies grew more solid with every breath, while physical sensations of arousal prickled their skin and genitals. Each of their energy centers started to spin in a circular motion. All energy centers had to be open, connected, and spinning before the couple could usher in the energy of the soul-in-waiting.

When they felt as though their bodies would explode with the ecstatically high vibrations of love and reception, the man gently eased himself into the woman, and sat still again. Intercourse involved almost no movement, except a slight rocking. They gave and received energy, until they erupted in a mutual orgasm of body and soul. Then they entered into a deep, peaceful sleep, still entwined around each other. After awakening from his blissful sleep, the man withdrew, and the process would begin again with another man.

After two weeks of mating ceremonies, the midwives examined the woman to verify pregnancy. This procedure was only a formality, because a couple knew instantly when the woman had become impregnated. Although everyone knew who the father was, we refrained from discussing it. The child wasn't a possession and didn't belong to the birth parents, but rather was a member of our entire community. When pregnancy was confirmed, visitations from the men stopped and life returned to normal in the village except for the new mother-to-be.

Each member of the community was an integral part of the pregnancy and birth process, and they celebrated their successful union. Each looked forward to the arrival of the child as both an individual and collective achievement. The entire village was pregnant, ecstatically anticipating the arrival of a new being.

Joyfully and lovingly, we continued to provide for the mother. Throughout the nine months of pregnancy and for as long as two years afterwards, all food and necessities were furnished to the mother by the community. During the period of isolated pregnancy, the Council of Elders continually sent Gold Light and energy to the mother, and kept her safe and cherished in our collective hearts.

During pregnancy, the mother focused on nurturing the soul coming in through meditating and bonding with the baby. At the same time she concentrated on her physical body and health, ate a selected diet, and maintained a fairly stringent physical regimen of walking and physical activity.

Remaining alone in physical form for such a long period was difficult for the new mother. So villagers, midwives, and healers voluntarily took turns submerging into physical form to stay with her, to help her maintain connection to the community and Source. They went on walks and swam with her, massaged and stroked her. The midwives taught her physical and mental exercises that she could utilize during labor and birth.

The last three months involved bonding the unborn into the vibrations of each member of the community. The mother spent time in each community member's home to acquaint the unborn with those individuals. She also visited the Council of Elders, to select a date and time for the actual birth. They jointly communicated with the soul to prepare the child for its emergence and separation from the womb. The birthing mother gave notice to let the villagers know when birth was imminent and the conch was blown to alert us.

A special birthing place was created by the villagers, out in the fresh air but covered with a thatched roof supported by poles. Underneath we dug a large hole in the ground, an "Earthwomb," and lined it with soft fibrous bark and fronds from palm trees, weaving the material so the Earthwomb became watertight. We filled it with sacred water and Gold Light, then floated fragrant flower petals of ylang ylang, plumeria, and white ginger as well as healing herbs. The leaves, herbs, and flowers used in this ritual were aromatic and beautiful, as well as analgesic and antiseptic to promote healing. We carefully placed crystals around the edge of the new fertile Earthwomb. Artists drew sacred symbols on the ground around the birthing place who had previously carved symbols into the poles supporting the roof.

The purpose of the Earthwomb was to allow the infant to recover from its separation from the mother, while bonding with nature and the other villagers. Floating in warm sacred water, while feeling the connection to others, our baby would feel secure. Additionally, the Earthwomb was a secure "water bed" for the welcoming ritual.

Now we were ready to bring the mother-to-be to the sacred birthing waters. Several men went to the mother's home and helped her onto a stretcher, attached to two bamboo poles for carrying and supporting her, lovingly woven with the softest and strongest fibers. And so she was carried to the holy birthplace. All of us sat on the ground around the Earthwomb, many holding hands, encircling her with our deepest love and gratitude. We invited our bird and animal friends to come into the circle and participate. Often villagers from other communities would trek for days or weeks to attend the all-important event, bringing presents for the child, the birth mother and our community. Indeed, everyone was present for this auspicious occasion.

Musicians played; everyone toned and sang ever so sweetly to soothe the mother and sang songs of welcome for the new child. The Elders invoked the Gold Light to surround us all. The midwives gently massaged the mother, and adorned her with crystals, while she entered into an altered state of deeply ecstatic anticipation.

Birthing was effortless and painless because of her physical exercises. The woman had also been trained to shift her consciousness, and detach herself from her body while still being energetically connected to herself and the baby. Like a whoosh of warm energy, the infant came through the birth canal and emerged into the water of the Earthwomb. Because of the woman's ability to expand her uterus, cervix, and vagina to accommodate the birth, forceful cutting or manipulation was generally unnecessary. The new baby was brought to the surface of the water and laid on the mother's stomach. Each of us took our turn welcoming the new baby by touching the child and beaming a reception of love and light. The healers and midwives bathed the mother while the new infant lay on her stomach, and allowed the afterbirth to wash out into the sacred waters. The umbilical cord was not cut until it had stopped pulsing and the baby was breathing fully on its own. Our newborn child learned trust and surrender immediately.

Two Elders crossed arms and carefully joined hands under the baby to gently support it, floating in the water. Our new mother was then helped out of the water and laid down on the soft stretcher near her child, joining with the rest of the village. Her bleeding was minimal, and healing was practically instantaneous.

A Lemurian Baptism (Sacred Ritual)

The Elders' job was to engage all of the baby's senses. They closed their eyes and hummed. This sacred sound was meant not only to activate the baby's hearing and to calm it but also to integrate the vibration of the physical body with its light body. They were resolute to make our sacred young one's passage into a physical body whole and integrated in the most soothing, effortless way. The Elders also activated, aligned, attuned, and linked the vibration of the infant's body with that of the villagers, the universe, and nature. While the baby floated in the warm, buoyant, golden earthwomb supported by the two Elders, other Elders in a highly altered state began the sacred birth ceremony known as the Sacred Becoming Ritual. They touched and activated each of the energy centers on the baby's body to infuse them with Gold Light, comforting the baby so it wouldn't reject its new body. (This activation of energy centers is more fully described in chapter 6.) The ethereal dimension where the baby came from was vastly easier to exist in, and they wanted the baby to accept the new form of being. Later the afterbirth was taken to a ceremonial place in the village square and offered to the Earth as a source of nourishment. We burned the mother's hut that had been specially built outside the community and she rejoined her family. Afterwards, of course, we had a huge celebration. Although many women were never honored to be chosen as mothers in their lifetimes, they didn't feel slighted, ignored or considered second best. The same held true for the men of our villages. Once a woman gave birth, only rarely was she selected again.

Chapter Four

Childhood: The Communal Lap

There were no unwanted children in Lemuria. Each precious child was carefully planned for, welcomed, adored, and lovingly raised. Being raised in our environment was like a fairy tale, an enchanted land of earthly fairy godmothers and godfathers. The birth of a single child occurred infrequently, spaced from ten up to one hundred years apart in each community. Following birth the mother breast-fed, then surrendered the newborn to the Council of Elders for the "Becoming" ritual. At that time many of the women of the village also began to lactate and took turns feeding the baby. This was done because the child was a member of our entire community, and belonged to no one set of parents. Although a child was born to an individual mother, the community parented the child from the beginning of its life to emancipation from childhood. All men and women of a community were the child's enraptured parents.

We knew that during the first two years of a child's life the baby was only loosely connected to its physical body. So we took turns holding our sweet infant who was never isolated or abandoned, never even laid down. Our child slept, ate, cuddled, played with, and was held on the "communal lap" of men, women, and older children. This way our child would fully integrate a physical body while also maintaining a light body. When the tot was ready to crawl or walk, he or she was encouraged to do so, only returning to someone's lap to rest, sleep or cuddle. Consequently, there were no crib deaths in Lemuria, no orphans, no birth or separation trauma, and no worn-out parents.

43

The forming of this deep connection with the community nurtured the full bloom of a child's personal nature, talents, and being. Connections formed in the first two years molded our children's characters, bonded them to the community, and supported their growing awareness of their innate gifts and Universal Wisdom. We knew the value of carefully and gently raising a beloved child.

Much attention was given to each growing infant in the first two years, a full-time joyful celebration of the delivery of a new life. Our children were lovingly guarded, protected, caressed, and nurtured. Infants received daily massages and were gently bathed in waterfalls, streams, and oceans, made to feel at one with nature. This treatment was to ensure that they were grounded in their bodies while becoming bonded with nature, the community, and the source of all being.

Raising our growing and developing children was the most fun-filled, awe-inspiring, and fulfilling responsibility we could imagine. By observing and nourishing a child's true essence, wisdom, and connectedness to all, we breathed life into that child. We never made the mistake of imposing our personal aspirations on our children. Each child's soul had already declared its purpose and intentions for coming into our world. Everyone in the community knew about the influence of the sun, moon, planets, and stars, and how to support our child's talents and gifts. Our Council of Elders observed the child frequently and paid attention to the parenting taking place. They didn't directly participate in the parenting, but were the child's overall protectors and guides. They could step in and correct something that was not proceeding in the child's best interest and for the highest good of all. They made certain that the village parented the child with the best possible attitudes, unconditional love, and sacredness of spirit.

The child received abundant suckling from humans and nature. We were always in contact with the baby's body by touching, massaging, cuddling, stroking, and bathing. We added plumeria, ylang ylang, and fresh herbs to our baby's bath water for absorption of healing essences. The child learned the Lemurian Way through our playful and loving interactions.

The child was so filled with love and nurturing that there wasn't an instant of hunger or unfulfilled need. Yet we encouraged our child's natural rhythm to ensure that the tot would stay connected to its own body wisdom, while being provided for abundantly.

Mothers stopped lactating and nursing when a child was about two years old. Prior to that we offered finger foods like fruit and other natural foods. A two-year ritual was performed at this time. The transition was an important one, from being continually held and breast-fed to learning a sense of self-responsibility; learning about the food of life and eating from the table of nature; nurturing oneself and not depending wholly on others; exploring inner wisdom, self-awareness and learning how to care for one's own needs. However, we continued to communally parent our children for many years. Our toddlers were also taught chanting, singing, and dancing. Our little children were inspired to use their Source-given ability of communicating telepathically. We raised them with nature so they easily imitated sounds of birds, animals, and dolphins. Around the time that modern children are throwing tantrums, our children rode dolphins with playful ease, buoyant in their light bodies. Babysitting Elders cast Gold Light around babies and communicated with predators, to align with protecting our precious children.

Our children began their formal education around two years old in Universal Wisdom and Dolphin Brain patterning. In Light Temples the accelerated vibration was very high. Inside the Light Temple one could know everything that was in the universe, while being acutely aware of Universal Wisdom. Teachers took our children there to learn how to teleport their light bodies to other planets, galaxies, and dimensions, as well as to other places on Earth through the energy grids. They also further developed telepathic communication and psychic awareness. Children also learned how to work with crystals. Light Temples generated information and comprehension quickly. The teachers brought along those who were storytellers and libraries, who assisted the children to integrate knowledge and Universal Wisdom. Going to the ocean was part of the educational process in Lemurian communities near the ocean. Sometimes inland communities brought their children there as well. The children not only rode on dolphins, but also communicated with them in the dolphin language, and were taken to dolphin chambers. Dolphin chambers were Light Temples at energy grids underwater and were connected to Sirius and other galaxies in the universe, as well as to Creator Source. Since we were unable to breathe underwater like our dolphin friends, we either floated on the surface of the water or lay on the beach in an altered state of consciousness while dolphins communicated with us telepathically.

Dolphins intuitively access information as a whole. So they were loving and joyful teachers and storytellers for our children as well as libraries of highly evolved information. Our children learned how to integrate information from them.

At communities further inland our children went to mountaintops, waterfalls, and into the forest to learn. Teachers led them to Light Temples on the top of mountains that were flooded with the same Golden Light as dolphin chambers.

Teachers helped the children to learn about nature around them and in every living creature. The children also spent time with crafts people, to watch, absorb, and play with their own creative expression. Our children also observed everyone within the context of daily life, to get a sense of the harmony and interweaving of the whole community.

A Rite of Passage was performed between seven and eleven years old, depending on a child's readiness and individual maturity. Children were honored with a ritual as they began apprenticeship for their life's work, predestined before conception. Life's work was a source of joy, creativity, playfulness, and a gift to the community. Children would be very excited when selected to begin their life's work. At that point they moved in to study with a master of the trade they would practice. Their apprenticeship didn't detract from the playfulness of childhood, but was an added expression of fun. Over the next ten to twenty years, they lived with each of the masters of their trade in their home village, learning skills they would practice for the rest of their long and fruitful lives.

At approximately fifteen years old, adolescents were initiated into a full sexual life through a sacred sex ritual during a fire ceremony. Prior to that, they experienced lovemaking by playing at sex by touching, cuddling, kissing, fondling, and stroking each other.

We knew then, as you do today, that children were our society's most precious asset, and we honored them accordingly. They were the ones who would perpetuate our indispensable Lemurian skills, knowledge, Universal Wisdom, and our loving communal spirit.

Children are sacred.

Bless the children. Honor their spirit. Children want to love and be loved. Live and let live. Give and be received. Look into the wonder of a child's spirit as you would a playful dolphin, a cuddly kitten, or a budding fruit tree you planted from seed. Because they look to you for loving protection and caring affection, know that you have the ability to open or close that little child's precious spirit. Give them your heart.

Children are not our possessions. They are a gift from the Universe. To plan for the birth of a child is to understand the wisdom of divine timing and creation, for the highest good of all. Listen to your higher self, to Creator Source, and ask if the time is correct for bringing another soul to Earth and into your care. Children are from Creator Source, just as we all are. They are only entrusted to us to be cared for, but they don't belong to us. Give them freedom. Listen to the children.

You seek love? Allow children to easily fill you from the deep well of their trusting hearts, the same love they give to a new kitten or puppy. You seek joy? Go to the park and observe the children. Let them teach you their wonderful and wacky sense of humor and joy. Give them your childishness. Children are our teachers. Open your mind to them. Your greatest task is to surrender to their teachings. They are transmitters of Universal Wisdom. They know what wisdom is. They live there. Let your children lead you into your own wisdom. They are here to evolve the planet in consciousness, just as you were for your parents. Give them your mind. Teach the children. Children want to learn. They crave knowledge through their awe of the universe. See the world through the wonder of children's eyes. Embrace their inquisitive nature. Take them on journeys of the heart, to magical kingdoms of the mind. Share the wonders of the world with them. Watch them grow through their imagination and the joy of wonderment. Allow them to soar into the aliveness and joy of creation. Give them your soul.—The Elders

Chapter Five

Love is the Glue

Creative work was one of our most beloved, exciting, fun-filled activities in which we indulged ourselves throughout an entire lifetime. We immersed ourselves in our special life's work with passion, excitement, and joy. Work was creative play—something that each of us did because our talents, abilities, indeed our very existence was drawn towards that particular activity. Because we lived such long lives, we never had the feeling that we left anything undone or unfinished; our work was always in progress.

And yet you might ask—were we bored? Hardly ever. Our work was a natural extension of our individualities. Our whole heart and soul yearned for our work. Our whole being (and our community) was nurtured by our work. We lived our work. We loved our work. Ate, slept, and drank our work. We were inseparable from our work. Our work was us.

Prior to incarnation, we already had our own abilities, gifts, talents, distinctive likes, and dislikes. Consequently, our work was chosen before conception, based on our soul's personality. Our work was our identity. Not only was our work connected to the soul's gifts and talents, the sort of work we loved to do best, but it was aligned with the needs of our community. If our community needed another healer, a healer soul was chosen before the mating rituals began. If our community required another singer, we chose a soul who loved to sing, and so on. Of course, we were always free to learn and perform other jobs and we sometimes aspired to learn new occupations. None of us really

49

knew another trade from the inside of our skin the way we knew our life's work, but it was fun to learn other skills. However, we loved our work, our most cherished activity, as well as our gift to honor ourselves and our community.

Jobs included woodworkers, crystal workers, builders, food gatherers, decorators, midwives, dancers, singers, musicians, storytellers, artists, herbalists, makers of sacred products like flower essences and essential oils, healers, teachers, elders, and many others. We'll discuss a few of those jobs below.

Libraries

Libraries were people who easily and compactly stored and kept all information intact, including Universal Wisdom inside their bodies. Libraries also kept the chronology of all people on the land of Lemuria, along with the knowledge of all jobs. When we wanted to learn or know something quickly, we went to a Library to access what we wanted. Our Libraries had information categorized much like a computer system in a modern library. However, their memories were stored, not in books or other records, but in their bodies and spirits. If one Library was not available, another could be of assistance, since each Library contained all information. Dolphins and whales were also Libraries, and they could telepathically swap information with human Libraries. Elders often needed to access information, so they interlinked and interconnected with Libraries. Many jobs in our civilization were interwoven with each other.

Storytellers

Storytellers were in charge of narrating Lemurian history, because they accessed information from the Libraries. Libraries didn't tell stories, but merely collected information, while the Storytellers "read the Libraries' books" and told the stories. Consequently Librarians and Storytellers worked together quite closely. Furthermore, Storytellers could read the stories and information in stones, crystals, and nature. Each Storyteller could recite the complete history of Lemuria, all persons living and dead, their jobs, and any interesting stories. Their task was not merely informative but also to entertain. They were especially adept at converting Universal Wisdom into stories that were easy to understand as well as highly interesting.

Sacred Council of Elders

One of the most vital jobs in our civilization was that of an Elder. Elders embodied a high degree of integrity and wisdom, regardless of age, and they were highly respected. Elders were held in supreme regard and acknowledged for their special gifts. However, they weren't in power over us, but aligned for the good of all Lemurians. Although their jobs were quite important, they had no pride or egotism, only a humble acceptance of their function. All of us had access to Universal Wisdom, but we chose to give full responsibility to our Elders, to ease our daily life when a decision affected the whole.

These men and women were specially educated and trained as youngsters by current Elders in reading the heavens, "holding" the vision and energy of Lemuria, the land, the people, and our connection to Creator Source and Universal Wisdom. Elders also assisted healers in re-creation and regeneration of physical and light bodies. Elders assisted in the death process, kept grids aligned as Earth plates shifted, and could read the energy of the stars and planets for proper timing of important events.

As we have discussed, they consulted with the cosmos and Creator Source regarding availability of new souls and communicated with potential souls to be added to our communities. They discerned the appropriate time for conception and birth. They selected a mother for that soul (with Creator Source and the soul's assistance) and the men who would procreate with the mother-to-be.

They helped to maintain Light Temples. The Elders were responsible to communicate with the stars and planets, and to keep the light expressway in Light Temples open for people to travel inter-globally, inter-galactically, and inter-dimensionally. Elders met at the center of the six-pointed star, in the Holy of Holy Light Temple to keep each other clear and focused, to regenerate Lemurian energy for the continent, to access Universal Wisdom and to make joint decisions that would affect all Lemurians. Some Elders chose to die and reincarnate into dolphin bodies and while continuing their jobs while being in a dolphin form. Thus, many dolphins were actually Lemurian Elders, which is still true today. Elder incarnation into dolphin bodies was one of the reasons we held dolphins in the same high regard as their human counterparts. Some Elders who ended physical incarnations became known as Ascended Masters.

Healers

The Healers worked quite closely with the Elders. They were responsible, by invoking Gold Light and Universal Wisdom to work its magic, to regenerate and re-create our physical bodies, rejuvenate our Light Bodies, assist the midwives at birth, and support those who were choosing to leave the physical body entirely. Upon a few occasions the Healers also attended to accidental injury and could perform psychic surgery and spiritual healing. Illness was rare in Lemuria because Healers rejuvenated the physical body with preventative measures before illness took hold. Healers knew how to employ the healing and revitalizing energy of plants, herbs, water, crystals, Light, flowers, beetles, and touch. Thus, Healers worked closely with Elders, Gardeners, crystal workers, and those creating sacred essences of herbs and flowers.

Gardeners

The Gardeners propagated and fertilized native plants with Light using crystals to amplify the process. Consequently, the vegetation in and around our communities was lush and healthy. Even being around plants was a healing and joyful experience. They especially tended with considerable care all plants that we ate. Gardeners also observed nature, and used her methods of using decaying and decomposing matter as fertilizer.

Furthermore the Gardeners' job was open communication with all of the plants. The Gardeners knew that all plants were equal partners with the community. No flower, herb, vegetable or fruit was picked without permission from the plant.

Gardeners worked closely with Healers, to nurture the healing plants and flowers and advise of the proper time to harvest. Gardeners worked closely with those who manufactured flower and herbal essences, sacred potions, and healing oils.

Teachers

Everyone could be a teacher for the young, according to their talent and profession, their best and most loved creative expression. We also had specially trained Teachers. They took the children to Dolphin Chambers under the water, and to our Light Temples, where information and Universal Wisdom was disseminated. Our children learned telepathic skills and other psychic abilities. They taught children how to travel inter-planetarily, inter-galactically, and inter-dimensionally.

Teachers not only taught the young but all our citizens; our education continued throughout our lives. Teachers worked closely with Libraries and Storytellers. Dolphins were also teachers.

Musicians, Singers, Dancers, and Artists

Since our vibrations came through Venus, art, dancing, and music were very important to us. Creating was not just an artistic task, but a spiritual one as well. Artistic jobs were especially meaningful because we revered beauty, harmony, and creative expression. Creative artists devoted their lives to creating pleasure, joy, and fun through the arts.

Music was important in all our rituals and our Musicians developed musical instruments for rituals that imitated both the sound of nature and the universe. Their musical instruments included wind chimes, wooden instruments, stringed instruments including a small harp, flutes, drums, and the conch shell. The conch was used at the end of a ritual. Musicians composed and played music of all kinds, from joyous to devotional, and also invoking the kundalini for sexual play, sexual initiation, and the all-important mating ritual. Musicians also played their instruments for celebrations and just for the fun of it.

Musicians accompanied the Singers, although sometimes they sang a capella. Our Singers were skilled in an extensive vocal range.

Both Musicians and Singers were an important part of all rituals and celebrations. They knew the importance of sacred sound and tones. Singers also chanted, along with the entire community, during rituals and healings. Although some people devoted their lives to singing, singing was a pastime that all Lemurians freely participated in. The Sacred words and sounds of our songs and chants deepened Universal Wisdom and invoked healing and regeneration. Dancers were also involved in rituals and celebrations. While the whole community usually danced at these times, the Dancers would lead them in ritual dance, yet sometimes danced alone. Dancers also accompanied Storytellers, dancing the stories of the cosmos, Universal heritage and the history of our civilization. All Lemurians created beautiful objects, decorated their homes and their communities, adorned themselves and each other, polished and carved wooden bowls and stone and other wooden objects, and collected shells and crystals. Artists were members of the community whose life's work was to create art objects. Artists were important in all phases of our daily life and we had many different kinds. Some worked with wood. Other carved in stone. Yet others wove and made cloth, especially the Gold Light cloth that was so important in our rituals. Some artists made decorative objects and jewelry out of seashells and crystals. A few Artists became interior designers. Others built our homes. Artists also carved and drew the Sacred Symbols that were a meaningful part of our Light Temples.

Crystal Workers

Crystals were friends in our communities. Crystal Workers held a special reverence for our crystalline friends and knew them intimately. The Crystal Workers searched for crystals and knew each crystal's special vibration and how to activate the crystal's inherent knowledge and ability. Crystal Workers had extensive knowledge of how to use crystals. They also knew how to implant Lemurian wisdom into crystals, so that the crystals became living "books" for anyone who could read them. Crystals were used in our homes, in all rituals, childbirth, and in our Light Temples.

Crystal Workers worked closely with Elders, Healers, and Artists.

Creators of Healing Essences

Manufacturers of healing essences created special elixirs and potions using herbs, flowers, roots, crystals, Gold Light, and other natural ingredients. These important and highly effective distillations were used in all rituals, for healing and regeneration of the physical body as well as to activate and increase learning. Creators of healing essences worked closely with Elders, Healers, and Gardeners. The use of healing essences has been remembered and practiced throughout much of human history. In modern times, those are known as herbs, flower essences, essential oils, crystal elixirs, aura soma, and many other forms.

These jobs are just a few of those included in Lemuria. No job was regarded as better or less than any other, regardless of the job description. All work was considered important, vital to the smooth operation of each community and the generation of creativity in each individual as well as important to our lifestyle.

Everyone's true essence was apparent in his or her work. Thus our Lemurian lifestyle was harmoniously held together, in part, because our community was supported by members' enjoyment in expressing their gifts, abilities, and talents through their work.

Chapter Six

Sacred Sound and Language

We intuited that sound is the causal tuning fork of the universe, so sound was highly sacred and important to us. Because sound was instrumental in the creation of the Universe ("In the beginning was the Word"), we knew that sound connected us to the Universe and to each other. Sound, we discovered, has the power to:

Create—We manifested rocks, crystals, and other objects "out of thin air," organizing atoms into materialization, using specific pitches, vibrations, and tones.

Manipulate—We could move and affect large and small objects using sound, known as telekinesis. We could also alter certain qualities of inanimate form, make larger, smaller, lighter, denser, and so on by making particular sounds. We could also dematerialize and rematerialize (move) huge objects like rocks and tree trunks using certain sounds.

Summon animals and people—We mimicked dolphins, whales, birds, animals, and insects in order to call them to us. Drumming was used for multiple types of long and short-distance messages. The conch was blown to alert us to important information and for announcements.

Inspire—We used sounds in many forms: singing, chanting, and toning, musical instruments, and drumming in celebrations, meditations, rituals, ceremonies, and in everyday life. The sounds of animals were sacred, so we imitated these by growling, roaring, shouting, whistling, and humming. The natural sounds of Earth were inspirational to us and we reproduced the sounds of wind, rain, thunder, water, and fire with our musical instruments and voices.

We could hear the musical vibrations of the Angelic and Higher Realms and imitated what we heard. Our singers and musicians were especially good at replicating astral music. Musicians developed musical instruments to closely duplicate both the sound of nature and the celestial spheres. These included wind chimes, wooden instruments, stringed instruments including a small harp, flutes, and drums. The conch shell, blown three times, was used to signal the end of a ritual.

Particular sounds were used to invoke Gold Light and spiritual enlightenment by singing, chanting, and toning. Toning is still used in some religions; for example, Gregorian chants as mantras such as the mantra "om," and to a lesser degree in hymns. Some Buddhist monks retain the ability to combine two tones into one with their voices to intone a highly sacred sound.

Nurture—We used singing, toning, and chanting during healings and to regenerate our physical bodies. Our Elders hummed at childbirth, to soothe the newborn child and to integrate its physical body with the Earth energy and its spiritual body. Laughter was a sacred sound and we knew how to have fun, play, experience happiness, joy and ecstasy. Completely uninhibited, our merriment, giggling and laughter could be heard from far away.

Heal—The vibration of laughter could also heal ailments (disease) in the physical body. We utilized sound by singing, chanting, and toning during healings and to regenerate our physical bodies. Singing, chanting, and toning were vital to keep our energy centers attuned, aligned, and open, especially those in the throat, forehead, and solar plexus and to generate and activate our light bodies.

Communicate—Our rudimentary language combined simple but sacred vibratory sounds. Many were high-pitched; some were beyond the normal hearing of most humans. Our language contained tonal inflections, which sounded like musical notes. When we spoke, we almost sounded as if we were singing. Some words sounded like buzzing, others like rippling water. Often words sounded like what they represented. Many of our simple words could impart a different meaning when intoned in a slightly different way, similar to the modern Vietnamese language.

Words were comprised of mostly vowels, like many Polynesian languages today. Our language used simple words but each sound within a word was sacred and powerful, similar to Hebrew according to the Kabbalah. In fact, Hebrew and ancient West Indian languages contain remnants of our Lemurian language with its attendant force and meaning.

Our vocabulary was limited. However, although our words seemed simple, our language was not. Our words were comprised of many meanings joined together, to express a complex idea. The Hawaiian language captures some of the quality of Lemurian language. For example, the word Hawai'i is made up of three ideas—ha (breath), wa (sea), and ii (air).

Destroy—Certain sounds could destroy (dematerialize) material objects as well as create disharmony, illness, dissension, unhappiness, and conflict in human bodies and spirits. Thus, we were prudent and deliberate when making sounds. Many of your so-called negative words had no equivalent or translation in our language. Words like fear, greed, selfishness, hate, war, pride, possession, and jealousy, among many others, were not part of our language because these concepts didn't exist in our society. The few negative Lemurian words we had could all be loosely translated: "disharmony" or "creates an unpleasant feeling in the body."

Since language uses sacred sound and is extremely powerful, we used language sparingly and consciously. We rarely spoke anyway since we were telepathic, and could communicate thoughts, ideas, wants, and needs nonverbally. Certain occasions, especially our rituals, called for language. When foreigners visited us from outside Lemuria, we reverted to speaking, as opposed to our usual telepathic communication, out of courtesy. However, our language was exceptionally difficult to understand, learn, reproduce, and articulate for non-Lemurians. In order to hear and speak our language, one had to be in a light body to discern some of the more higher pitched sounds and subtle tonal variations of the words. We were uncomfortable with visitors from other lands who needed to converse at great length. Much of what they said we intuited as distortions, exaggerations or sometimes outright lies.

Intention—We used language in the form of prayers and goals, both spoken and unspoken, to facilitate and manifest our intentions.

Entertainment—Sound and language were also a form of play, for diversion and entertainment in our celebrations and festivals.

Lovemaking—We would sometimes employ sound and language in lovemaking. For us, sound, through the composition of singing, crooning, or toning, was a form of lovemaking.

Music, chanting, singing, toning, and language employed the use of sacred sounds in multiple forms. Although these appeared elementary to outsiders, they were practiced in intricate ways for intelligent, meaningful, and significant purposes, especially in our rituals.

Sacred Symbols

We had no written language you would understand today. We carved and drew sacred symbols instead. These symbols did not express our spoken language per se, but were created for a much different reason. To the uninitiated observer, these symbols appeared meaningless, unsophisticated, overly simplistic, perhaps even primitive. But to us, they were a means to a greater and holy end. Each symbol contained vast meaning, similar to Egyptian hieroglyphics, as a representation of an idea. Furthermore, each symbol didn't merely stand for something, but acted as a "doorway" to higher understanding, and we often meditated on a symbol for clarity, wisdom, and insight. Our symbols were also meant to awaken and activate power when gazing at them and were used as a means to focus this power as well. Sacred symbols were carved or drawn on everything; painted on faces and bodies, depicted on clothing, incorporated into our homes, and carved on pillars of wood and on slabs we formed from hardened clay.

Chapter Seven

Sacred Sites

As we said earlier, we created Gold Light Temples, which were designed to operate at maximum efficiency throughout all time at energy stations on grids around our Motherland. Often these grids were situated on or near natural energy vortices of certain rock formations, mountaintops, or holy wells.

The concentrated vibrations from our holy Light Temples extended about a mile in diameter in every direction. However, Light Temples required energy to maintain their ability to be fully functioning. So Temples were situated in places where specific vortices of energy were generated from the body of Mother Earth. Since the sun, moon, planets, and stars transmitted energy fields, the Temples were aligned with those as well.

We constructed our Light Temples out of Light, sacred sound, energy, thought, intention, and vibration. We intuited that the universe resonates at a high level to sacred geometric forms, and so we created our Temples with that in mind. Thus they appeared as three-dimensional structures shaped like pyramids. If you recall our discussion of six-pointed stars, we discussed how triangles were sacred symbols to us. In a Light Temple, each of the four sides of the Temple's pyramid was an equilateral triangle, a sacred geometric configuration.

However, even though a Temple looked real to the casual observer, it wasn't solid, but an ephemeral illusion. If outsiders touched a Temple "wall," they were surprised to find that their fingers moved through it as if it were composed of mist. Yet from inside a Temple one could see without the illusion of walls outside into the abundance of nature beyond, because flowers, trees, and plants grew lavishly up to its edges, their development having been encouraged by the vibrations, light, and energy.

Birds, insects, and animals, too, were drawn to the energy of our Light Temples and performed their own sacred ceremonies of mating, birth, and death within its enclosure. We respected our fellow creatures and allowed them free access to our Temples, feeling honored when they appeared. Sometimes we found animal predators and their prey peacefully coexisting within our Temples for brief periods, as though the sympathetic vibrations were harmonizing them as well. Furthermore, like us, they sensed the sacred nature of the Temples and refrained from despoiling the enclosure or living within its boundaries. We created a mosaic floor for our Temples out of crystals of all types, colors, sizes, and shapes, often in geometric designs or sacred symbols. We dug holes and planted columns of wooden beams cut from tree trunks, usually sandalwood or rosewood, around the foundation. These posts were intended to support the shimmering golden cloth canopy, so gossamer that sunlight could shine through it. The beams were intricately carved with sacred symbols, especially the symbol of the spider web and concentric circles or spirals, which represented our connection to each other and the universe as well as Creator Source. In the center of the Temple was a carved and decorated four-foot-high wooden pole, on top of which we placed a solid gold bowl, especially made for the Temple by our craftspeople. This golden bowl, a potent conductor of energy, was filled with sacred water, herbs, flowers, and crystals, a highly effective mixture for healing and other purposes. When we performed rituals within a Light Temple, we brought soft mattresses with us to lay upon.

Sometimes we placed massive rocks, rich in crystalline composition around the perimeter of the Temple grounds, forming a circular or oval arrangement of "standing stones," in alignment with both terrestrial and extraterrestrial energies. We Lemurians could move these heavy objects with our minds, group synergy and intention, often called telekinesis, so transporting large objects was no problem for us.

Sound (coupled with intention) was another method we used to pick up and move rocks, boulders, and trees. Sound also can destroy. Joshua in the Christian Bible story used sound to obliterate the walls of Jericho, but we never used sound in that way. We could also form rocks and crystals by organizing chemical composition through intentional sacred sounds and mold it into solid objects like rocks and crystals, as though we were "singing" matter into being. Another way we could transport objects was by dematerializing dense matter from one place then rematerializing it in another.

Our Light Temples fulfilled a number of functions: healing of illness and disease (inharmonious feelings in our bodies); regeneration and re-creation of physical and light bodies; and our all-important rituals. We also used our Light Temples for telepathic communication throughout our communities, the planet and entire universe, for travel in our light bodies throughout the cosmos as well as to other times and dimensions. Light Temples in that regard were portals or doorways into other realities. We also used our Temples for ongoing learning of and instruction in so-called psychic abilities and Universal Laws and Wisdom.

Within our Temples we accessed both energy from Earthly and heavenly sources as well as traveled in our light bodies along pathways of energy to wellsprings of dynamism and creativity found in the cosmos. We invoked Gold Light to hold the tremendous energies in place and to continuously strengthen the exalted vibrations contained in them. Because we intended our Temples as holy and sacred, our reverence for them further contained the energies therein. Without our Light Temples, life in Lemuria as we knew it was unmanageable and undesirable. Light Temples literally kept us alive and healthy for hundreds, even thousands of years. Using knowledge gained from our Temples integrated our civilization into a harmonious oneness, reminded us of our spiritual roots, and furthered our integration of wisdom. What we accomplished appeared miraculous by others' standards. Other civilizations copied our knowledge and tried to duplicate our techniques of implanting light and energy into their own sacred sites on Earth's grids and energy centers. However, they were never able to create temples out of light, nor could they accomplish changing nonorganic material into organic the way we could. They did discover how to deposit information, coding, and descriptions into rock and stone. Atlanteans and other civilizations understood how to utilize crystals and the immense power that could be generated through their use. The Atlanteans liked the colossal feeling of our Temples and sought to replicate the enormous energy with rock and earth. Thus they and their descendants created huge edifices that still stand today. Stonehenge and the Egyptian pyramids are two of many such structures that utilized Lemurian know-how by future civilizations. Subsequent religions built edifices upon old sites because they intuited the energies there. Unfortunately, much of the wisdom and original intentions of Light Temples have fragmented and passed into obscurity, or were protected as secret for millennia. You may think that our ability to construct and utilize Light Temples is a mad fantasy or a fictional myth. However, if you visit sacred sites in existence today, you can experience firsthand the awesome monuments that were inspired by Lemurian intelligence. You may experience some of the portals to other dimensions and times, connect with wisdom and knowledge, and encounter healing energies that continue to pour through these sacred sites. Furthermore, it is our belief that sacred sites are beginning to light up and beckon modern people to visit for spiritual and psychic illumination. If you should feel such a "call," we hope that you can travel there either in your physical body or in consciousness.

Chapter Eight

Time, Life Span, and Death: Time is of the Essence

Looking at clocks and calendars was meaningless in Lemuria. Time was primarily based on living in each moment. We followed the flow of life as we felt it in both our physical and light bodies. We also respected the Earth's body time as well as the sun, moon, planets, and stars. These were our guides, and we trusted, honored, and interpreted their cycles. Yet, paradoxically, time moved very quickly for us. Because of the swift movement of time, we lived to be quite old, which generated myths of immortality. We were able to spend hundreds or thousands of years in one body due to many factors.

We lived in light bodies, whose vibrations were faster and less substantial than ordinary physical matter. We occupied these light bodies most of the time except to eat, eliminate, mate, create art objects, and other earth-bound activities. We were able to physically re-enter dense bodies and remain in that state by an act of conscious will, known as intention, but we did so infrequently. Imagine that our physical bodies were like new cars, that were kept parked in the garage most of the time, while we "drove" our light bodies. Our "vehicles" wouldn't wear out as fast. Now imagine that our vehicles were more like plants than machines, and with nurturing, could last as long as there was sunlight, air, water, and nutrients to sustain them. Because of our high vibratory rate and multidimensional lifestyle, time for us was speeded up and passed much faster than in modern times.

We utilized our Light Temples to regenerate and re-create the physical body. Light Temples, as we have said before, are placed on huge energy vortices connected to Earth, as well as aligned with extraterrestrial and other dimensional forces, and further intensified by our group synergy. Within our Light Temples we received Gold Light. This light recreated the body blueprint of DNA, initiating and integrating, recreating and generating new cells, as though we were born again, but into our same body. Healers and Elders assisted us when using Light Temples.

We employed group synergy and group thought, which helped us stay established in light bodies, as well as withstand the rigors of physical form.

We were connected to Mother Earth, which provided energy to help regenerate and nurture our physical bodies. In essence, we were connected to and fostered by the timeless, gentle energy of our Lemurian land. We lived in present time, based on inner connectedness and awareness of what was needed in each moment. We followed the dictates of our bodies and intuition.

We rested when tired, ate when hungry, made love when wanting to connect in that way, created when inspired, and so on. We could stop what we were doing, and immediately give our attention to something more interesting—a party, making love, performing a healing, etc. We lived in the flow of life as we felt it in our bodies and in the Earth body, seasons, and animals. Mating, birth, and death rituals were the only items we preplanned. As we lived joyfully in each present moment, shifting gears without hesitation, we created a sense of timelessness. This kind of fully living in each present moment, while listening to one's intuition, makes time go very fast. Present-moment living also lessens the strain on the physical body; in fact, it rejuvenates the body.

We knew the importance of play and fun. Often our jobs would go undone in order to fulfill our need to play. Play, as we've said before, is akin to Light, which accelerated time and made us younger. Much of our "timelessness" was spent being connected to each other in loving vibrational energy, receiving huge doses of time-less Golden Light.

Death Ritual

We could detach from our bodies, travel inter-galactically or inter-dimension-ally, and oscillate at different vibrations at will, all the while remaining con-nected to our physical bodies. We could also choose to permanently leave our physical body, which you call death. Death of our physical bodies was due to will, or rather a desire to leave that body. However you want to look at it, dying was merely a choice, the result of receiving a message that it was time for us to depart. All members of the community intuited the appropriateness of our leaving as well and wholeheartedly supported our decision. When we felt that message, we then consulted with the Council of Elders, who would consult the heavens, reading the energy of the stars and planets, for an appro-priate date and time for our departure.

Choosing to leave our beloved community was a major decision. Once severing the connection to and departing from our physical bodies, we couldn't reverse the process. We weren't allowed to be reborn back into Lemuria either. Millions of souls petitioned to join Lemuria; very few of them were selected. So once we left, there was no going back. We could choose to be reborn into another place and time on Earth, however. Some opted to become dolphins. Others returned to the stars, other dimensions and vibrations, or the spirit world.

We didn't see our death as an end, but merely a step through the doorway of the universe, into a different existence, but without the constraints of a physical body. Because our spirit self was immortal, we weren't afraid. No one mourned our death; leaving for a new life was cause for celebration. And be-cause we knew we were all connected forever, there were no tearful good-byes. The community had a wonderful, joyful festival prior to our death ritual, with feasting, dancing, and singing. Members of other communities would also travel long distances to participate in the joyful occasion.

After our celebration we proceeded to a nearby Light Temple, where our death rituals were always held. As with all other sacred rituals, crystals were enlisted to help with the process of beaming light and energy. The entire com-munity and visitors attended while animal friends were also invited. Our Lemurian brothers and sisters circled the Light Temple, singing and playing instruments. We chanted a sacred song, while Gold Light was invoked and encircled us all.

The individual lay down in the center of the Light Temple on a comfortable pallet. Our Elders and Healers sat close by, meditating on and visualizing the Gold Light, asking Creator Source to help make the transition smooth. The person relaxed, letting the soul easily slip out of the body, as practiced throughout a lifetime. Then they asked that the energy cord, which connected the soul to the body, be severed. Once severed, our dear Lemurian friend was gone, painlessly, effortlessly, in a matter of moments.

Lauren's Death

I was only an adolescent, about 800 years old, when I chose to die. I had been a dancer and storyteller. I mostly told stories by dancing, rather than speaking, although I did learn the stories verbatim. I was lighthearted but careless, and tended not to watch where I was going. One day I was dancing around the high mountain forest, not paying attention to the precipice looming behind me. I accidentally fell down a tall cliff, shattering the bones in my legs, and breaking my hips, back, and neck. I sent a telepathic message to advise the community of my plight. I went into an altered state, which dissipated any pain. When the Healers found me, I was unable to move my legs, and several broken vertebrae were poking through my skin. They worked with me for what seemed a long time but were able to heal my body. When they were finished, the Healers gently advised me that I would walk again but weren't sure how graceful I would be or if I would be able to dance as before.

I listened to their kind words but felt dismay. Dancing was my life's work. What if I couldn't dance anymore? I made an immediate decision and left my body, severing the cord. This was an unusual, not to mention abrupt, way for a Lemurian to depart, but I was (and still am) impulsive. I left without the joyous celebration and sweet ritual with my friends that were part of our Lemurian Way and still regret it.

Once departed, I realized my mistake, but couldn't return. My next two lives were spent in Atlantis, before moving on to many others.

Chapter Nine

The Atlanteans

Each land area on Earth has its own energy field, a specific "personality" which tends to affect the people living there. Differing energy fields alter the vibrations of bodies of humans living there and their group psychology, as well as their emotional and spiritual progress.

Because the Atlanteans lived in their own unique energy field, they developed differently from us Lemurians and thus had different interests. Atlantis, especially the western half of the continent, contained a fiery, restless energy leading to an intense curiosity. Their feeling of impatience led them to exploration and inventiveness. They developed an amazing ability to navigate and developed tools and a primitive technology very early in their civilization.

Our energy, on the other hand, was more person- and home-oriented, resulting in an overwhelming preoccupation with relationships and group activity, rather than expansion. We strived to experience total connection to Creator Source, Universal Laws, and Wisdom, and a wholly supportive, interlinking collective consciousness. We were content, peaceful, joyful, and fun-loving, with no desire to change the status quo. Our Lemurian culture and civilization flourished for tens of thousands of years, yet modern people might consider our lifestyle as stagnant. When we reached a certain level of contentment, comfort, and harmony, outer progress stopped. So when the Atlanteans discovered us, they may have considered US to be backward, lazy, boring, technologically inferior, even stupid. We noticed the Atlanteans talked a lot. Their talking hurt our ears and our hearts. Furthermore, they often didn't say what they meant, or mean what they said. Because of mutual language barriers, combined with our joyful giggling and laughter, we must have seemed like babbling children to them.

The Atlanteans began their civilization connected to Universal Wisdom and each other, just as we did. Unfortunately, they fell out of their light bodies into physical form later in their development, as did many of the human species. Afterwards they retained a collective unconscious, permeated with Universal Wisdom, for thousands of years, which only fragmented again after the massive destructive of their civilization. However, long before discovering Lemuria, their incomplete understanding of Universal Wisdom had become materialistic, with some members of their society possessing the desire to control nature and each other.

Since Lemurians were spiritually inclined and non-possessive, we freely shared. We were not only willing, but eager to share with the Atlanteans. Because we liked to teach, we happily taught them, not only Universal Wisdom and Laws, but also sacred geometry, the energy of stars and planets, crystals, nurturing plants, essential oil production, herbal lore, and how to create beautiful art and cloth objects.

We appreciated how difficult it was for them to understand our abilities without our point of reference and invoked Gold Light to help them assimilate our knowledge. However, although many understood, some turned away from our good intentions. Consequently, those Atlanteans thought we weren't much more than primitive savages, who were weak enough to give away valuable information, knowledge, wisdom, and possessions for free. Yet the huge body of Universal Wisdom we effortlessly maintained intrigued them, and later became their obsession.

The Atlanteans happily absorbed huge segments of information from us and transplanted it into their own society. Because Atlanteans were technologically inclined, they implemented the knowledge they gleaned from us in practical ways. They used our friends, the crystals, as tools in their technology. They created ships that could sail in the air as well as on and under the sea, and used crystal energy to operate their vessels, a form of power to heat, cool, and provide lighting and energy, and utilized our ability to excavate and move objects easily. They used our understanding of sacred geometry to create temples, buildings, and marvelously constructed cities.

Confusion exists in ancient clay tablets, other records, and myths about our ability to create fantastic buildings, cities, and monuments. But these weren't our doing. We simply knew about sacred geometry, grids, and energy stations and possessed what might be called higher mathematics and engineering. These were implemented by other people, mainly Atlanteans. We were neither shipbuilders nor colonizers. These all were accomplished by non-Lemurians, although we could be considered the architects and engineers for such wonders. The Atlanteans also attempted to copy our facility to use thought forms, energy grids, and telepathy to communicate with each other, infuse information in objects and areas of land travel out-of-body, promote longevity, and locate their own energy grids. Unfortunately, they didn't understand the original intent of higher knowledge and the power that accompanied it, nor did they seem to intend it for the betterment of all. Because some of them hungered for power, they used knowledge for personal gain and to skillfully manipulate people. The Atlanteans learned our facility to read the heavens, although not entirely understanding what they were reading or why. In the process of imitating us, they created many monuments to the stars, sun, and moon. Other civilizations learned these abilities as well, sometimes copying from the Atlanteans. However, like the children's game of "telephone," precious knowledge became garbled, disjointed, and pieces were lost in the process.

We Lemurians were connected to Universal Wisdom with the assistance of our Council of Elders. As you may remember, our Elders made decisions based on their job of keeping us connected to the light. But the Atlanteans misunderstood our Elders' position in the Lemurian society to be one of power. They created priest/kings who were initiated into the Wisdom, which they made secret, instead of sharing Wisdom with all Atlantean and colonized citizens. Because jealousy and possessiveness didn't exist, we were comfortable with multiple sex partners. The Atlanteans were confused and judgmental about our sexual practices, although they didn't hesitate to find sex partners among us. Later on, the product of their sexual exploration resulted in babies that were part Lemurian and part Atlantean. The mix of our two societies lowered our total Lemurian vibration, which later contributed to our collapse.

Visitors from Atlantis traveled to Lemuria for centuries, trading and learning. They even set up colonies on our homeland. We asked that their colonies be situated in areas other than on our grids and remain contained in those regions, which they consented to do at first. However, a few were unable to stay within their own territories, and they began making overtures to our Elders, to spread out even further. Our Elders refused, which led to animosity from those Atlanteans.

After many centuries of peaceful coexistence, some Atlanteans began capturing unwilling Lemurians and taking them away from our homeland. When we were enslaved or captured by Atlanteans, they not only took us to Atlantis but to colonies in Tibet, Egypt, the Middle East, parts of Europe, Africa, and South America.

Although we could and did travel extensively within Lemuria, we never desired to, nor were capable of journeying outside our beloved continent. Leaving the precious energy of our homeland and fellow Lemurians was like a death knell, producing the myth of Shangri La. We never left our country willingly, because leaving our land led us to being forced into a totally physical existence, without being able to fully sustain our spiritual body and group connection. Without our sacred temples, Elders, healers, and the synergy of other Lemurians, we simply couldn't maintain our light body nor regenerate our physical one. Not only that, but without our precious land energy of cooperation and unconditional love, we began to take on the energy of whatever land we were brought to. We either died, or assumed a dense physical form with a greatly shortened life span and a dismal attitude. Similarly, an Australian Aborigine often died in his jail cell when imprisoned.

However, we brought with us our knowledge, experience, and memories. The amazing stories we told of our homeland became myths and legends, while our knowledge was eagerly assimilated by other civilizations.

Experimentation

Late in our history, some misguided Atlantean scientists took us captive, to help them augment their technology and teach them how to use the power of crystals, and unfortunately to perform experiments on those who survived the trip to Atlantis. The Atlanteans wanted to know how our brains worked, how we performed telepathically, and how we accessed information. They greatly admired our abilities and wanted to tap into it for their own technological and scientific gain. Atlanteans found that our Elders and Healers made the best subjects, since they worked extensively with light energies, other dimensions, stars, and planets. However, our civilization became devastated with the loss of so many Elders and Healers. Those Atlantean scientists implanted crystals, sometimes in the chest (heart chakra), the middle of our forehead (third eye) and sometimes in the womb. This crystal was used to control and attract us through beaming light from other crystals to us, sometimes from atop pyramidal-shaped buildings. The Atlanteans knew we transferred knowledge into crystals, so they transplanted various crystals into fellow Atlanteans as well to test their abilities.

Because we could attune our bodies to dolphins and other animals, they experimented, injecting animal sperm into us, similar to artificial insemination. They thought if they impregnated us, we would become a mixture of human and animal The results of these experiments created hideous organisms, and led to myths of centaurs, satyrs, and other half-human creatures.

They wanted to discover how we could live in altered, highly vibrational, light bodies while maintaining human form and so performed dissections and autopsies on us to discover our secret.

Other experiments done by the Atlanteans included placing us great distances apart to see how and at what distance we communicated telepathically. Then they performed surgery on our brains, sometimes even when we were still alive! They wanted to see if they removed part of our brain, whether our telepathic ability still existed. They would remove a part of our brain and place a crystal there to see if it duplicated our mind.

They also tried transplanting our brains into Atlanteans, to see if they could simulate telepathy and other abilities. They performed other experiments on their own people to see if they could get Atlantean brains to work like ours did.

All these experiments failed. They succeeded only in killing our bodies. The scientists never discovered how we operated, even when we lovingly explained our knowledge to them. They were misguided, thinking our brains were the source of our knowledge, which they never understood, even after centuries of testing. Our brains weren't bringing forth knowledge. It arose out of the energy of our precious land, our group consciousness, and our connection to Universal Wisdom.

What the scientists also failed to comprehend was that information came to us synergistically as a group. We knew we were connected to each other, and used Universal Wisdom in group concert for the good of all, whereas the Atlanteans didn't utilize their group mind in this way.

We treasured Universal Wisdom as sacred. Wisdom was a gift from Creator God and we treated it reverently and utilized it lovingly. We also understood higher knowledge as a whole, whereas the Atlanteans focused on each individual part of it. Granted, the Atlanteans could utilize those bits and pieces, but they had difficulty replicating the body of higher knowledge.

Bless the Atlanteans. We don't mean to imply they were evil people. Most of them were good and kindly souls. They started out as we did, in the Light. They struggled to understand, grow, and learn in their physical bodies, too. Their society included those who practiced higher knowledge and wisdom also. But the dark impulse towards power and control was highly seductive and overwhelmed many of them long after we had become a faint memory.

Chapter Ten

The End of a Golden Age

I saw cliffs in the middle of the valleys [in New Zealand] that once were situated at the edge of the ocean or sea. I saw departing spirits that walked through this valley to the sea. Did the Lemurians become dolphins or just leave the planet? Why did we Lemurians choose to fall from this life of love and light? Or did we choose it? Were we destroyed out of our nonviolence in a world that seemed to relish violence? Did love fail us? We must have chosen to surrender our lives at some level. Maybe it was too painful to stay any longer. Or maybe our work on the planet was done. Maybe we wanted to experience the process of becoming conscious of other emotions and compassion, to understand the Atlanteans and other lost souls. Or maybe we chose to leave because there was too much attack on our culture. Did psychic bombardment cause us to lose our connection to our divinity and the power of love? Did Atlantean experiments with the weather cause the fall of our culture? Did they attack us out of their fear of our powers?"

  —Journal entry, Sareya Orion, Feb. 14, 1997, New Zealand

A number of factors led to the death of our civilization. Young Gaia was having growing pains. Our Motherland's tectonic plates were shifting and submerging under each other, making the Earth's crust buckle, heave, and crack. Consequently we experienced stronger and more frequent Earthquakes, tidal waves, and volcanic activity. Soon, we intuited, our homeland would be completely destroyed.

75

Our people fled from the trembling continent, seeking refuge in other lands; scattering like dry leaves on a fall day; taking Wisdom and knowledge of the Lemurian Way with them as well-worn luggage. This flight from our homeland is incorporated into myths and knowledge in many cultures.

Some prepared to live underground, in caves, to wait out the destruction. Other Lemurians "died" and entered into dolphin bodies. Some of us returned home to other galaxies, dimensions or spirit planes.

Still other Lemurians returned to Earth in physical form but in other civilizations. We felt we could learn, experience, and have compassion for those who lived in separation from each other and Universal Wisdom, and to continue to learn about the body and emotions.

Our precious Lemurian energy was being decimated and split asunder in other ways. A large number of our Elders, Libraries, and Healers had been captured into slavery by the Atlantean scientists. Their absence diminished us and made us feel lost, like a sailboat on a still day. Our youngest people were the most affected by this loss.

Furthermore, they were attracted by the Atlantean life of glamour and a "civilized" society. They left our simple settlements for the magnificent cities the Atlantean had created on our continent. The temptation was too great for young souls not fully embodied into the Lemurian Way. The Atlantean also taught them to cultivate food and domesticate animals to eat.

Our former friends of the animal and plant kingdom were overwhelmed by our children's desire for specific foods to appease their newly-whetted physical appetites. Intrigued by the Atlantean' unlimited ability to talk, our young ones began to lose their telepathic abilities and intuitive discernment.

Furthermore, many of our people were intermarrying with Atlantean and other visitors to our continent. The more we intermarried, the lower our Lemurian vibration became. However, with the massive changes taking place, no Lemurian was ever judged or criticized for marrying an outsider. We held meetings to steel ourselves for the dire consequences: living fully in a physical body, lower vibration children, and subsequent diminishing of our group consciousness. Yet we left the final decision up to each individual and his/her desire and conscience.

The vibration of the entire planet was becoming denser and less filled with light. Darkness penetrated into Lemuria, lowering our vibration, too. Emanations of Gold Light began to diminish everywhere on the planet, as well as in Lemuria. Our Light Temples, once sacred and holy "schools of learning," were being overrun by foreigners who wanted to have a quick and easy "fix" of wisdom. We became more and more despondent, feeling the vibration shifting always downward. Universal Wisdom continued to diminish and fragment, threatening to become a dim memory in humankind's glorious past.

Before complete destruction could occur, concerned that the Light would be extinguished forever, we gathered in our Temples and formulated messages as Light and Thought which we broadcast to the planet's intelligence. We concentrated on those groups and individuals whom we believed could retain and comprehend the vast knowledge and beamed our messages to them.

We also put messages in crystals and shipped them inter-dimensionally using sound and intention to different parts of the globe, much as a shipwrecked sailor puts a letter in a bottle. We also deposited records in crystals, rocks, and stone already in existence throughout the planet. Some of the crystals are known as "record keepers." We prayed and intended for Wisdom to be saved, understood, and cherished until such time as the pieces could be put back together.

We grieved over our civilization's failure, especially our Elders. They saw our failure as twofold.

- We had avoided becoming completely physical for fear of becoming earthbound, thus failing to accomplish our task—living fully in physical bodies.

- We were unable to raise the level of planetary consciousness so that all Earth's inhabitants could access Universal Wisdom and live the Lemurian Way.

We Elders have continued our job over eons of time, guiding and whispering our messages to those who could or would hear. We feel that human consciousness is now at a critical juncture in evolution and can incorporate the spiritual into the physical.

Message from the Elders

"We are the Lemurian Elders. You know us by many names. None of them are important. What is important is the message. The message is 'we failed.' We lost our golden opportunity to become fully integrated into body and soul.

Now it is your turn.

We are counting on you.

We are the messengers. We bring you Good News. The time of change is now.

The dogs bark but no one listens. The cats cry for their kittens, but they are grown. The whales sing their songs, but is there anyone left who can hear?

You can hear now. Please hear us and consider what we say. Take this message into your heart. Feel it. Know that you are an important link in getting the message out."

Lemurian Connection

When our civilization died, our links to each other and Universal Wisdom were severed. But broken links can be bonded, and all people can be adjoined to the family of light once again. Connection to Universal Wisdom can also be restored. Human souls have the capability to reintroduce those connections. Furthermore, those of you alive today need to know a vital piece of information: You are already immersed in physical form. You've accomplished that which we Lemurians were unable or unwilling to do. Your only remaining goal is to reclaim your divinity, your spiritual heritage, your essential nature, to retrieve that most precious part of you. This is easy. And we're here to help, to remind you. In Part II we share with you our knowledge, to help revive precious Wisdom and Connection, to attain what you've always known you could do.

Part II

Chapter Eleven

Overview: Living the Lemurian Way

We Lemurians understood and strove to live as equal partners with the cosmos. In the history of earthly human existence, we experienced the most harmonious of all civilizations known to humankind.

We knew that Universal Wisdom and Universal Law are the most sacred and holy ingredients which constitute the universe. When embodying Universal Wisdom and Law into our society, we reaped the benefits of:

Unconditional love

Joy

Peace

A sense of connectedness to self, others, and Creator Source

Loving and truthful communication

Harmony with the entire living universe

Respecting intuitive feelings and knowledge

Happily performing jobs that come from unique talents.

As we've said before, we weren't perfect—but we had a perfect system. We knew how the universe works and put that information into practice. We were skilled in rising above petty differences in order to achieve unity with each other and all creation.

So why did we fail? We Lemurians failed because we were afraid, afraid to become completely human, to completely inhabit human bodies. We were afraid that, by becoming human, we would lose our Divine connection. We failed to realize that to be human, while accessing Universal Wisdom and Universal Law, was our task. But we stubbornly refused and our civilization died out. So the task remains unfinished. The challenge of being totally human while simultaneously wholly divine is still to be met. We, as Lemurian Elders, recognize our failure and have continued to stay in communication with your planet, to guide and clarify, sharing what we have learned. The Lemurian Way hasn't died, but is alive, ever-present and growing tremendously in modern human consciousness.

Many of you who directly experienced lifetimes in Lemuria keenly feel the failure, and desire to expand yourselves in order to bring peace, harmony, and joy to yourselves and each other. Those who never lived in Lemuria nevertheless contain memories of wisdom and knowledge in your deepest hearts, and work to elevate the consciousness of the planet and yourselves.

People throughout the ages have retained elements of the Lemurian Way through myths, archetypes, collective unconscious, religions, in philosophy, in individual and group souls. All human beings sense the natural state of spiritual life, as well as Creator Source and Gold Light. This innate knowingness is evident in many qualities and aspects of human life today:

The desire to parent more lovingly and consciously

The desire to resolve conflict through peaceful means

The explosion of psychic and spiritual awareness, books, and workshops

The expansion of religions

The search for meaning and God

The desire for individual, group, and planetary peace

The desire for play and the discontent of working in unfulfilling jobs

The discontent with the status quo, resulting in people separating from the system

The desire to travel to sacred sites

The desire for freedom and equality

The desire to know one's purpose and share talents and gifts freely

The desire to have one's talents and gifts acknowledged as valuable

The desire to understand Universal Wisdom

The desire to understand and incorporate ancient mystical teachings

The desire to eat healthfully and lead more healthy lifestyles

The interest in spiritual healing

A yearning to live in harmony with the planet and to clean up water, air, and land pollution, and to use healthy farming methods

Re-emergence of the Goddess religion and ideas

An increased interest in dolphins, angels, and UFOs

Creation of smaller communities and healing retreat centers

The desire to create peaceful, cooperative, and loving relationships

In sum, the search for our essential nature, a "return" home

Paradoxically we can go home at any time, like Dorothy in The Wizard of Oz, who possessed the ruby slippers. But the process of searching leads one to greater understanding and wisdom. Had Dorothy missed the adventure through "Oz." she might have failed to know her courage, her heart, and her brain. Thus the process of learning is as important as the goal. So perhaps what we Lemurian Elders define as "failure" was merely an important step in the human adventure.

Part II will explain how we utilized the tools of Universal Wisdom and Law, which we call the Lemurian Way. These tools are not exclusively ours, but belong to everyone at all times. We won't tell you anything new, but will describe the tools in meaningful, lucid descriptions, sharing with you what we've learned, and describing our experience of the Universe in an orderly, concrete, but simple manner.

Only one roadblock stands in your way: amnesia. We present our understanding of Universal Law and Wisdom to help awaken memories sleeping in DNA for everyone, not just a select few. Our purpose is to ignite your deepest memories into a brush fire of recognition and excitement, in order for you to exhume your genius lying buried just beneath the surface.

Responsibility

No individual or single group has all of the pieces of knowledge. Pieces are to be found in Individuals and groups around the world, making connection on a global scale imperative.

Every individual has a special, unique key to the door of the "Gates of Heaven." The door has many locks, and one is required to unlock his or her part of it. Each special key is comprised of one's talents, desires, understandings, unique visions, abilities, individual precognition, and recognition of truth and wisdom.

Everyone's key is vital in order for every other key to fit in the universal lock. No one is exempt. The Founding Fathers of the United States brought to life a vital Lemurian principle: "everyone is created equal": from Presidents to homeless people on the street; from scintillating movie stars to the quiet audience in the theater; from Pope, ministers, and other spiritual leaders to every atheist; from corporate billionaires to each mother and child on welfare; from Mother Theresa to terrorists. Everyone moves to their own dance on the Earth and every dance is perfect, no matter what it looks like.

As one presents a key into the lock, it makes room for other keys to fit, which makes unlocking the door easier for the next person. And the next. And the next. No one can get through the Gates of Heaven unless everyone goes through together. We, the Elders, need you. We ask for way-showers, who are willing to pass on Universal Wisdom, both verbally and non-verbally. We ask you to present your key and unlock your part of the door, so that you and your entire planet Earth can live the Lemurian Way.

Chapter Twelve

Bodywise

*"Listen to your body" was a gentle yet constant reminder to each of us
in Lemuria, to feel and experience every moment.
Our bodies were essential tools to living the Lemurian Way.*

Mind versus Intellect

A human body contains intelligence that we will call the "mind." The Greek word for mind is menos, spirit, which conveys the meaning we attribute to mind. This spirit is a complex of elements that feels, perceives, senses, and wills on all levels and dimensions. The body, which contains this mind, is attuned to Universal Laws, Truth, and Wisdom.

Mind is different from intellect. Intellect, from the Latin intellectus, means to understand and reason, as distinguished from feeling; it has the capacity for knowledge and thought and can be attached to ego.

Body/Mind

The mind and body, then, are unified oneness, connected and attuned to Universal Law and Wisdom. We will call this the body/mind, which is wise beyond imagination. Every person on Earth contains one. "Heart" or "soul" can be used interchangeably for body/mind.

The body/mind is attached directly in a vibrational pathway to one's authentic identity or Higher Self, which is immutably connected to Creator Source. All messages received in the body/mind are in actuality messages from the Higher Self, which knows what lessons we are here to learn and what direction we need to take at any given time to accomplish our goals. The body/mind knows and feels what is right for us. The body/mind, then, is a sacred receptacle for higher knowledge and instructions, on a level so vast the intellect can't comprehend it. Therefore, in order to evolve, we must listen to our body/minds. To ignore body/mind messages are to ignore one's Higher Self, and consequently Creator Source.

The body/mind has the capacity to access personal and global priorities, lessons, memories, knowledge, ideas, and inventions that originate from the evolving, expanding universe in the form of perceptions, notions, visions, and flashes of insight. That was why we Lemurians were considered psychic. Certain kinds of dreams and insights received just before going to sleep or upon awakening are often messages from the body/mind. Because thoughts and ideas are universal, no one body/mind is truly inventive or original; it is merely tuned in to universal wavelengths.

In addition, the body/mind acts like a transmitter to send messages, to will or intend a certain outcome, goal, desire, or creation. Because the body/mind is ultimately connected to one's Higher Self and Creator Source, these desires and goals belong to our Higher Self and ultimately Creator Source. In other words, the Creator Source wants what we want. When we passionately feel to create, the passion to create as well as the image of creation has been passed along to us from our Higher Selves and Creator Source. When we have a desire, the desire is also Creator Source's desire. Therefore, all desires, goals, and creations are in everyone's best interest.

However, in order to actualize a goal or desire, one must "prime the pump." This means several things:

Follow-through action or activity is required, to let the universe know "you mean business."

A goal or desire must be retained strongly in the mind.

The goal must be as specific as possible.

The same is true of what we don't want, what we prefer to eliminate from our lives. These again are connected to our Higher Selves and Creator Source. Our body/minds instinctively and intuitively know impediments to personal and global growth, learning, and evolution. The body/mind is wise and receptive, while being connected to Universal Wisdom and intuitively connected to the Whole. Imagine that every individual body/mind is one piece of a gigantic universal jigsaw puzzle wherein each of the pieces fit together perfectly. That jigsaw puzzle contains all the elements of unified creation. The body/mind accesses its own piece of the puzzle, although it may not know how it fits with the other pieces of the puzzle or how all the pieces relate to each other. Yet body/mind wisdom, because it's connected to the whole puzzle, provides an exact fit. To respect body/mind wisdom is to honor the perfection of the working-out of the universal scheme of life.

The form a body/mind message takes depends on the individual, interpreted and translated into workable communication depending on one's main system of learning and assimilation. Some "feel" messages, while others see pictures. A third group may hear messages as words, phrases, or sentences. No method is better than any other. Does a composer hear messages as notes or musical compositions? Does a poet sense beat, measure, and rhyme? Are byte-sized computer language and symbols sensed by computer experts? Mathematicians in numbers? Possibly. These are the forms by which the composer, poet, computer expert, and mathematician make order of their individual universes. What is yours?

The body/mind is not judgmental. When one is accessing the body/mind, one looks at the world as a clean slate and senses the overall feelings and tone as experienced in the body. On the other hand, the intellect has preconceived thoughts. "A pink rose in full bloom" is a thought limited to the intellect. However, breathing in the rose's sweet scent, feeling the velvet texture of its petals, and seeing the well-formed perfection is body/mind perception.

We used many means to assist in connecting to and maintaining a body/mind union:

Meditation

Breathing in a connected way

Stretching

Exercise

Being out in nature

Eating healthy foods

Performing some new task, or an old one differently

Being creative

Games and sports

Swimming

Resting

Spiritual sex

Expressing oneself

Emotional clearing

But they all boiled down to: *listen* to what our body/mind was telling us, and *follow* its instructions.

Timing is an essential element. The body/mind is connected to Infinite Time, which means that the timing sensed in the body/mind is always correct. body/mind messages are received in present time, in the *now.*

The body/mind acts like a beacon, a neon light illuminating the path one is meant to follow. One's path can be analogous to a series of stepping stones; the stones into the future are hidden by dense undergrowth. First one steps on the stone being presented, lit up by the body/mind. As one steps on that stone on the path, the next stone lights up, and so on.

Often body/mind messages are fleeting, like a hummingbird sucking nectar from a flower, a fading sunset, a baby's first smile. We discovered that if we ignored the message, we missed a significant window of opportunity. Other times, vital communication from the body/mind persisted, becoming ever more insistent, more pressing, and louder until we listened and followed its instructions.

One's body/mind might desire an endeavor, goal, or project, but the execution of that goal may be intended for the future, as part of universal timing. In other words, timing is an inherent element in attaining goals. Meanwhile we could utilize our intellect to determine the "how" and "what" in executing that goal. Our body/minds would always let us know when the timing was right to begin (or end) a project.

Furthermore, we knew that each and every body/mind was connected to Creator Source, which made the body/mind an energy station filled with Gold Light. We realized there is no distinction between each body/mind and Creator Source. The body/mind and Creator Source are the same, indivisible and united. Each body/mind is an essential part of the entire jigsaw puzzle. Therefore, decisions corning from the wisdom of body/mind were always life-supporting and perfect, no matter what our intellect might try to convince us of otherwise.

Integrity is an important component of body/mind wisdom—to do that which one intuits is correct, regardless of whether anyone else is watching or not. Also integrity has to do with following a message even if we think it may affect someone else. Since the body/mind is connected to the Whole, it knows the perfection of the unity of all body/minds. So to avoid our body mind messages, thinking they will cause hurt or pain to someone else, creates disruption and disharmony in our core and in those around us.

The body/mind perceives, absorbs, intuits, and feels, whereas the intellect analyzes, compares, and judges. The intellect, when used inappropriately, is the source of duality, discontent, confusion, discouragement, jealousy, pride, possessiveness, and fear. We're not implying the intellect is a bad thing. The intellect has a very important job, to process information and to help with learning and understanding. The intellect also assists in locating and sorting through a variety of means to achieve goals. But intellectual denial can destroy, derail or mute spiritual experience and hamper the clarity of the body/mind. We Lemurians trained our intellects to function appropriately so they supported rather than hindered our body/mind wisdom and decisions.

The intellect may balk at a body/mind message, thinking "this can't be right; this doesn't make sense." But when we listened to and followed the body/mind instructions, results were truly amazing. And we didn't "should" on ourselves. If our intellect said we "should" do something, but our body/mind disagreed, our primary allegiance was to the body/mind.

We discovered that we could misinterpret feelings, emotions, or impulses that weren't body/mind wisdom of the highest order, but rather the intellect speaking. This discrepancy could be subtle, but important, and we strove and practiced to differentiate between body/mind messages and the intellect. We noticed what resulted after following a message. If the results didn't include harmony and peace for the self, then we knew we weren't accessing the body/mind.

A gut feeling, words or pictures from the body/mind may not make any sense to the intellect. We learned that following the intuition of our body/mind often boggled the intellect and brought on uncertainty. That was because the intellect had nothing tangible to cling to. Uncertainty was considered a good thing because it meant that we were firmly connected to the body/mind and only needed to loosen the intellect's tight rein over us.

The intellect's job is to sort through the vast array of information being received through the body/mind and make order out of it. When the intellect attempts to understand the information, it sometimes leads to confusion. The intellect tends to get overwhelmed—like dragging an elephant through a knot-hole. We learned to relax the intellect. How did we do that?

Stopped what we were doing. Breathed. Danced. Went out into nature. Stretched or exercised. Rested. Meditated. Remembered. Had fun! We found that play especially helped to relax the intellect. Were we irresponsible? Oh, no. We never worried that our work or chores would go undone. We became much more productive after we had allowed ourselves to take a play-break. Furthermore, fun and play have the same vibration as light, and the body and body/mind is activated and energized by light. By not having fun, we became disconnected from the body/mind, which created tiredness, boredom, discontent, anger, depression, etc. Even work was transformed into fun and play by finding the creative element, the part of work we loved. Fun creates joy, happiness, contentment, excitement, timelessness, creativity, and miracles. Sometimes cravings resulted when the physical body was out of balance. We were taught that cravings, as well as discomfort and pain, were illuminating messages from the body/mind to light up any thoughts, emotions or activities that were part of our learning process, and we paid attention. We tried to find the most healthful, loving, and creative solution for any particular problem.

The message we received might be vague, like "I'm bored" or "I'm tired." That was our signal to do something different. We tried various alternatives like "I could swim," or "I could visit a friend," or "I could rest," and paid attention to the results. Trial and error was the key to our success. We listened for the body's and body/mind's response to the question "How do I feel now?"

If we continued to respect the body/mind, we discovered the next step, after confusion, uncertainty, and feeling overwhelmed was transformation of thoughts, emotions, and situations to a harmonious level of being. When one experiences an "Aha!" this is a realization of the harmony of one's right action within the macrocosm of the universe, as the individual relates to the whole. When we followed body/mind intuitions, our bodies responded with relief, peace, and happiness. When honoring the body/mind and following its instructions, joy, contentment, and the ease of synchronistic events also took place. Miracles happened.

Whatever was right for one was not necessarily right for all. One's unique body/mind wisdom was the final authority for that individual. Only each individual could access his or her own body/mind. Therefore, others, including our Elders, had no right to assume they knew body/mind answers for anyone else or to impose their ideas on another.

We Elders were trained and skilled to allow knowing to take place by asking us, "What does your body/mind say to you?" Or questions like "What do you want?" or "How do you feel?" then listened to the answers, and fed back the synthesized responses to their clients. However, we went much further. When hearing an answer to our question, we received confirmation (or lack of it) by sensing how our body/minds felt. If the answer felt unclear or incorrect, we received a "no." If the answer was close, we began to feel tingling. If the answer was correct, we felt that "yes!" fully in our body/minds.

In the same way, our client sensed confirmation in his or her body/mind when we offered our synthesis, a "no," "maybe," or "yes." Thus, counseling sessions in Lemuria were merely a harmonious dance of body/minds.

We learned that living from the body/mind was like being securely held by Creator Source. Within Creator Source's arms, the body/mind became a divining rod for insight and discernment and led to feeling self-assured, happy, peaceful, loving, and joyful.

Chapter Thirteen

Universal Laws:
The Gold Light Canopy

We realized there is only one all-encompassing Universal Law: everything is connected to everything. This law has been in place at all times since creation and before. It is the glue which holds the universe together.

Imagine the universe as a giant canopy suffused with Gold Light that is connected and interconnected at all points. This canopy is a field of energy, vibration, and intelligence that includes physical and metaphysical laws. The universal canopy includes the entire manifestation of Creator Source—from the largest galaxy to the smallest particle, ourselves, our planet, nature, all living and inanimate things on it, plus other realms and dimensions including activity, thought, intention, and time. Moreover, all diverse parts of creation are unified with and related to one another within this manifestation. The Universe is similar to our Earth's ecosystem; disrupt one area and it affects all the others.

The Gold Light canopy is a cyclical canopy that loops back on itself like an endless figure eight. So everything connects to everything in an infinitely pulsing universe. "The universe breathed us and simultaneously we breathed the universe." Furthermore, the universal canopy is a dynamic organism, which means it's growing into higher and vaster orders of cohesion and evolution in an endlessly increasing loop, into higher and more harmonious structures, which also contain the parts. Thus, universal creation has no beginning and no end, but expands endlessly.

The nature of reality in the universal canopy is divine intelligence— everything has consciousness and a desire to grow, learn, and expand within its own realm of understanding. Everything is geared towards constant, continual, incessant, eternal, and steady learning, growth, development, and evolution. Learning in your physical being goes on ceaselessly, even in sleep. Sleep is needed to process what has been learned during the day and to integrate it into consciousness. The Higher Self is also processing eternally. Many tools exist for this learning—instinct, body/mind wisdom, experience, emotions, reincarnation, awareness, curiosity, the five senses, extrasensory perception, experimentation, and self-expression.

Within that Gold Light canopy we knew that human beings are multifaceted light stations, continuously transmitting and generating impulses through the field of energy, while merging with and receiving information. Consequently, thoughts, emotions, intentions, and actions are transmitted by this energy field throughout the entire canopy of the universe. In Lemuria we used the sacred symbol of a spider web to convey this principle. Because human beings are connected to the canopy, the energy of our thoughts, intentions, emotions, and actions reverberate throughout the universe. Thus, people send out signals that are clearly communicated. No matter what is said, how a person pretends, or how one tries to disguise and cover up, the truth bleeds through and can be sensed in another's body/mind.

Although we Lemurians were considered telepathic, in actuality we simply knew how this principle works. We learned how to check in with our body/minds to sense what essential communication was being transmitted and received. Consequently, secrets could not exist and lies were illusions. While everything was connected to us via the canopy, nothing belonged to us; we didn't own anything. Everything and every person in the universe were merely on loan to us for a specified period of time. So how did we "lease" what we wanted and desired?

The Law of Connection has a secondary component—the Law of Attraction. This law, also known as thought, is creative and was our mirror image "loan officer." Since we were connected to everything and everyone, every thought, act, desire, intention, and emotion cycled throughout the universe. Yet how we connected to everything, and who and what we attracted to ourselves was influenced by thoughts, emotions, intentions, and acts of everyone involved. The canopy is like a jigsaw puzzle in motion; all pieces of the puzzle fit and move together in a perfect amalgamation within the Gold Light canopy.

This Law of Attraction is in operation regardless of whether we are conscious or unconscious. When unconscious, one can pretend to be the "victim of the Universe." But when we Lemurians consciously lived within this law, we attracted more of what we desired. The outside world mirrored and aligned with us. Life became easier and we had more fun. We learned how to make friends with the Universe.

You've heard the phrase, opposites attract. That idea is the Law of Attraction working in harmony with the Law of Connection. We discovered that persons unlike ourselves (our mirror images) presented us with the greatest challenges; thus we could learn from them, grow, and expand. Our puzzle pieces matched perfectly, although not always congenially, and fit perfectly into the Gold canopy.

Because of these two laws, we recognized the responsibility of free will. What each of us thought and how each of us acted reverberated throughout creation. We knew we affected not only ourselves, but other people, the planet, and beyond. Therefore, we learned how to be affective in positive and harmonious ways—known as Universal Wisdom.

Chapter Fourteen

Threads of Universal Wisdom

We found it impossible to oppose living within the Gold Light canopy, to become disconnected or stop attracting. But we discovered one could spread disharmony and disruption throughout the canopy by vibrations of certain thoughts, emotions, and actions. Conversely, in order to harmonize with the universe, we learned about selective or higher vibrations—what we call Universal Wisdom.

Universal Wisdom consists of pieces yet is undivided at the same time, a complete system while containing parts of the system. Universal Wisdom is like a matrix of "gold threads" running through the canopy, yet the threads make up the "whole cloth." The threads of wisdom are complementary and naturally work together. Many of these threads loop back on each other and/or need each other to complete the circuit.

Universal Wisdom is voluntary, unlike Universal Laws of Connection and Attraction. We found Universal Wisdom can be employed consciously, unconsciously, partially, or even completely ignored. However, engaging even a small piece of Universal Wisdom promotes peace, harmony, happiness, joy, and a multitude of other wonderful qualities and furthers universal evolution. When we employed all of them as often as we could, the results were nothing less than miraculous.

Did we experience problems? Yes, sometimes. Weren't we perfect? No, not at all. We experienced disharmony enough to know it existed. So we thoroughly investigated and practiced Universal Wisdom in order to live in harmony.

How Did We Access Universal Wisdom?

All body/minds contain a "loom" on which to weave the threads of Universal Wisdom. In fact, this body/mind loom is extremely responsive to Universal Wisdom. In Lemuria we wove specific components of Universal Wisdom on our body/mind looms. What are these components? There are many of them, so we'll discuss only the most important and influential ones:

Intention
Forgiveness
Noticing (awareness)
Open and loving communication
Trust and surrender
Living in present time: Infinite Time
Acceptance and allowing
Gratitude
Detachment
Defenselessness
Giving and receiving
Respect
Joyful creation
Willingness
Empathy and compassion
Unconditional love
Mutual support

Karma and Grace

However, before we discuss the various threads of Universal Wisdom, we'd like to explain karma and grace—which are merely the Universal Laws of Connection and attraction in operation. The idea of karma is used in both Hinduism and Buddhism; however, the original concept came from us. What has generally been understood to be karma is really divided into two principles—karma and grace, which operate like stretching a rubber band. What expands out, comes back. Connection and Attraction is neither positive nor negative but merely mirrors thoughts, actions, intentions, and emotions. Like the physical law of gravity— if one throws a ball into the air, the ball will fall to Earth again. If one desires harmonious results (grace), one engages in harmonious thoughts and actions and ethical decisions. Grace can also include "miracles." When one initiates disharmonious thoughts and actions and unethical decisions, one receives disharmonious returns (karma). Karma exists in the intelligent universe so that individuals can learn from their mistakes. Most people at one time or another experience the gamut of karma—from merely challenging experiences to intense pain and suffering. Karmic lessons are universally acknowledged as undesirable. Yet both karma and grace are merely the action and reaction of Universal Laws, the ball bouncing back to Earth.

Intention

In Lemuria we found a way out of the "hell" of karma into the "heaven" of grace. One needed only to employ Universal Wisdom, the most powerful component of which is intention. Intending to learn from mistakes, to grow or to bring harmony to self and others exerts a far-reaching influence on other components of Universal Wisdom as well the Laws of Connection and Attraction, and leads to grace. Intention is a powerful thread of universal wisdom.

We'll give you an extreme example. If John Doe murders someone and he forgives himself, he can be absolved of his karmic "debt." But moving into a state of grace hinges on John Doe's intentions. Is he truly repentant? Does he intend to become a better person? Or is he trying to "con" the system? Is he forgiving himself, gaining a temporary reprieve, only to commit murder again? Universal Laws "read" John's intentions and resolve his karmic debt according to Connection and Attraction. Included in intention is consistent "right action." John Doe must consistently act like his intention, to behave like a better person, to act out his repentance. If John Doe forgives while intending to become a "good" person, harming no one else, and learning all personal lessons which provoked him to murder, he will ultimately actualize those intentions and find grace.

To intend an outcome, to keep a goal in mind, leads eventually to fulfillment of that goal because intention becomes a highly charged electromagnetic energy field which creates manifestations through the Laws of Attraction and Connection.

We also used intention as a vibrational, highly spiritual experience. We could actualize, cause things to happen or manifest because of our intense degree of focus of intention. Visualization contains an element of intention within it; however, intention is much more powerful than merely visualizing. We unfolded thought forms into existence. We created, out of nothingness by our willful concentration, to make something be. Our intention statement usually was in the form of "I have" followed by the specifics, asked of and as aligned with Creator Source. This form of intentional creation is highly evolved but can be learned by you in your three-dimensional world. How? One must become detached from any and all outcomes of one's personal life and wipe all personal desires and goals from the intellect. Then one can intend an outcome. Intention is greatly connected to the Laws of Connection and Attraction.

A Return to Karma for a Moment

But karma has much more to do with thought than action. Karma is powerfully created by how one thinks of oneself, either consciously or unconsciously, after a failure to take "right" action. We all have body/mind wisdom, which is connected to the canopy of Gold Light (Creator Source). Thus body/mind wisdom contains a universal conscience, the knowledge of right and wrong. This conscience knows when we have failed to take right action, either to oneself or another, which results in a "debt." The conscience draws up a contract to repay the debt and will not be satisfied until the debt is paid in full—in one form or another—through either unpleasant and painful karma, or grace. The karmic repayment may not be an exact replica of the original action and thought. John Doe may not necessarily be murdered in his next life, but his karmic debt could be repaid differently; for instance, by innocent imprisonment or confinement, insanity, paralysis, or suffering in some other form, or even by experiencing the murder of a loved one.

Forgiveness

Forgiveness, when combined with intention, easily pays off karmic debts and leads to a state of grace. Forgiveness, also known as absolution, is like mending a broken fence. Implicit in forgiveness is making amends or repairing what has been broken through wrong action. Making amends can simply be an apology, or it can involve taking a new right action. John Doe's amends may include a jail sentence; he might also choose to support the dependents of the person he murdered or perform community service. Making amends to those we have hurt, while pardoning them and ourselves for any failure to take right action, is the complete process of forgiveness. Forgiveness must be employed also when we judge another whom we believe has taken a wrong action (or failed to take right action).

We found that, without forgiveness, we lived in a world of hurt. We swam in a sea of pain, guilt, and judgment. Without forgiving ourselves or another, we created and prolonged physical, emotional, and mental pain, illness, dis-ease, unhappiness, and inharmonious relationships. We discovered only forgiveness, combined with intention, fully resolved the past, shifting us into right action and a state of grace. Without forgiveness and intention, we found we couldn't fully access the other facets of Universal Wisdom.

You may ask "But what about a good person who experiences many bad things?" If this person has completely forgiven self and others and still experiences bad things, then that person is not necessarily repaying karmic debts. The person's soul may have chosen a difficult path in order to learn valuable lessons while here on Earth, and preselects a tumultuous set of planetary configurations and particular events to accomplish that end. Their problems then are really gifts in disguise.

Furthermore, old souls who are in the process of completion often choose to be "conduits," providing community service by transmuting and transforming negative planetary energy into light, or grounding it into Mother Earth through their bodies, which can then appear as illness and other physical problems for the Conduit.

Noticing (Awareness)

Noticing is an extremely important expression of Universal Wisdom. We discovered that when we employed "noticing," as distinguished from judging and analyzing, we were in the appropriate mode for learning. Noticing aligns with body/mind wisdom called Awareness, while judging and analyzing comes from the intellect. Noticing is an important ingredient for learning, especially regarding correlations such as how we feel when we act a certain way; what occurs from others' actions; what happens when we follow body/mind wisdom. Noticing must employ detachment from judgments and analysis. Judging encouraged disharmony, separation, and disunity, while noticing brought about harmony, togetherness, and unity for us.

Open and Loving Communication

We knew that sound and words contained and generated power, while unspoken thoughts and emotions jammed energetic connection to self, others, and to wisdom. "Telling the truth" is a cleansing and clarifying process, which shifts negative energy and releases it to higher vibrations. Sound vibration also purifies and connects the throat and thymus centers with body/mind wisdom.

Without speaking our truth as we knew it, we created pain and uneasiness within ourselves. Furthermore, others felt and perceived all unspoken messages through their body/minds. To withhold speaking, or to say words incongruent with our thoughts and feelings created havoc, confusion, anger, and mistrust in those around us. When speaking our truth, the energy shifted from havoc to harmony, the air cleared and miracles happened.

There are two main components of open communication—loving intention and detachment. Loving means to communicate without blame, criticism, or judgment of self and others. Again, intention is the key to bringing harmony, understanding, clarity, and closeness to self and others. For example, if one communicates while intending the communication to be for the highest good, such as a more harmonious relationship, the intention will affect its own outcome. The second significant ingredient of communication is to be unattached to the outcome, to communicate without expecting a particular result.

"What about journaling and letter writing?" you may ask.

Journaling is a valuable tool to find out what a body/mind is wanting to communicate, and letters can communicate what you want to say. But journaling and letter writing alone won't clear an energy field like the spoken word. Open, loving, and truthful communication opened us up to more peace, joy, clarity, and harmony.

Trust and Surrender

At the very base of trust and surrender is Creator Source, who trusts our body/mind wisdom and surrenders our lives to us in free will. Trust and surrender are similar. Trust and surrender are both about relaxing the intellect and accessing body/mind wisdom. Trust is believing that one is taken care of and cared for by Creator Source, and that everything is perfect in the universal scheme of life. To trust is to be willing to leap off a cliff to the other side without evidence that the other side exists, to believe there's a landing pad even though it's nowhere in sight.

Trusting body/mind wisdom is like that of a baby bird. It has the instinct and inner knowing of how to fly. And, being a bird, its natural inclination is to fly. Trusting the universe to "allow" it to fly seems silly.

The same is true of human beings. We have the ability, the instinct, the knowing, the desire to "fly" in our own way. We only need to trust that we will be airborne once we leave the nest.

"Flying" is our natural heritage. Our own brilliance and ability is innate, inborn, instinctive, and permanently in place. We trained our children to trust themselves, while we trusted them as well. In awe we watched their lives unfold, observed our children's graceful flight, the effortless flap of wings, as the breeze of the universe caught them in its arms.

When we heard ourselves think or say "It's not fair!" or "If only..." we knew we weren't in surrender. Surrender was relaxing our need to be in control, to loosen our urgency to have what we wanted, when we wanted it. Surrender is also attached to Infinite Time (see section below). Surrender implies that life is perfect, and simply exists without meaning being attached to anything that happens along on our path. People, plants and animals, stones, atoms, thoughts, emotions, cars, houses, furniture, clothing, everything is vibration and energy that has no meaning, except the meaning contained within its own vibration and energy. The meaning of a cow is that it is a cow. The meaning of a chair is that it is a chair. The meaning of human beings is that they are human beings. The meaning of an atom is that it is an atom. The meaning of a thought is that it is a thought. All that exists is vibration and energy, part of the Universe, and as such it is not designed to harm us, bring us pain or pleasure; it merely exists.

Thus the search for meaning is meaningless but can disconnect us from others, Creator Source, and Universal Wisdom. When we are looking for meaning in life, paradoxically we are looking for what already exists within and around us. We are really searching for the means to access Universal Wisdom.

When searching for meaning, a danger lies in finding a piece of knowledge, then freezing it into selective meaning of a belief or ideology. We found that selective meaning is what the intellect mistakes for Wisdom, but is incongruent with Wisdom. Selective meaning implies that someone is "right" while another is "wrong." Selective meaning is what creates fear-based emotions like envy, possessiveness, anger, hate, revenge, and war. In Universal Wisdom, everyone is "right."

So we surrendered to the "What Is" of the universe and effortlessly moved with the natural flow of our lives, as connected to everything. The flow is not a direct one. It winds and meanders like a river; our job was to flow with the current. To stop surrendering, to fight the current, was to dam up the river. To go forward, to make progress and to learn is not always a straight line, not a linear process as the intellect understands it, but can be backwards, sideways, up and down, even around in circles. In surrender there was safety everywhere. Fear was unfounded. Despair was merely forgetfulness of life's perfection. Joy was ours. It existed within everyone's reach. We relaxed, trusted that the universe wholly loved and supported us, and surrendered to its magnificent flow. We also trusted ourselves to be wholly ourselves, trusted and surrendered to what our body/minds told us. Then we were cuddled on Creator Source's lap, which is large enough to hold all creation in radiant Gold Light.

Trust and surrender establishes a solid groundwork on which unconditional love, joy, and peaceful and harmonious relationships with self and others are built. Sometimes trust and surrender must be practiced over and over. Each time we trusted and surrendered, the more we were able to trust and surrender.

Time: Living in Present Time and Infinite Time

Time is connected to Universal Laws of Connection and Attraction in the physical world. Linear time is relative, based on these Universal Laws. Thus, time can seem to speed up, slow down, expand, and contract, while body/mind wisdom always operates in present time. In Lemuria we asked ourselves, "What do I feel or intuit right now?" Being in present time is the only way to fully access body/mind wisdom. When the body/mind sends a message, the message is intended for the present moment. However, the universe is constantly changing, growing, and evolving. Consequently the body/mind continues to send new messages at future "present times." Memories live in the past; goals, desires, and intentions are fulfilled in the future. But happiness only lives in the present.

Time is vast. Infinite Time is Creator Source's time, united with Universal Laws. We are always living in Infinite Time, which is synchronistic as connected to the jigsaw puzzle. People and events show up at the appropriate time in order for us to achieve our goals, dreams, and intentions. These will be delivered when all events and people have been perfectly arranged within Infinite Time. Living in Infinite Time requires patience, trust, and surrender.

Time, however, is meaningless and doesn't exist in the spirit realms. The spirit self is timeless and immortal. Thus, paradoxically, we became timeless beings by surrendering to Infinite Time.

Acceptance and Allowing

Each person, object, and event is precious and necessary in the overall jigsaw puzzle of life, in order for the universe to learn, grow, and evolve. Acceptance is about releasing our judgments, prejudices, or rejections of ourselves or another, or a situation, while believing it exists for the highest good of all, to know the "perfection" of the universe. In Lemuria no one pretended to know the answers (the piece of the puzzle) for another. To believe we did was arrogant and prideful. Thus it was unnecessary, presumptuous, antagonistic, and even impossible for us to try to "fix" another person or situation.

However, we discovered that we could "heal" difficulties, illness, and pain by allowing. Our Healers practiced *allowing*— being physically present with another while remaining open to any vibration (including Gold Light) and/or understanding (body/mind wisdom or Universal Wisdom)—to shift disharmony into harmony. Allowing is even more effective when teamed with intention. Allowing also applies to self-healing, which is akin to surrender. We found that acceptance and allowing dramatically transformed problems.

We're not implying that with either acceptance or surrender one should simply be passive to individual or global problems. We discovered that our body/mind wisdom would show us our particular path of right action.

Gratitude

All that happens is for the growth, learning, and evolution of ourselves and the universe. Pain and problems exist and are often necessary to advance learning and stimulate growth, especially in the third-dimensional world of planet Earth. Therefore, everything is significantly perfect regardless of how it looks to the intellect. To practice gratitude for everything (both positive and negative), and especially to be thankful out loud, is to increase one's universal bank account and to usher in grace.

Detachment

Detachment is to refrain from "taking things personally." We allowed others to have their own feelings, reactions, and "truth" and didn't try to protect others from our own body/mind messages as well. We knew that nothing and no one was intended to hurt us, nor were we intending to hurt others by standing firm in our body/mind wisdom. Lessons simply existed for our own and everyone else's growth, learning, and evolution, and as such had no meaning. Struggle wasn't a bad thing, but another step in evolution. All of life was a learning process, a giant schoolhouse.

So we became observers of our lives. We noticed what happened around us. We also detached from the need to help others who were struggling, except when asked or when our body/mind wisdom intervened, inviting us to assist. Everyone had a path to walk, as we had ours.

Furthermore, we practiced detachment when we achieved good things as well, which kept us from becoming arrogant, self-righteous, proud, and self-centered. We detached from judging the entire process of life and saw it as perfect.

Defenselessness and Neutrality

Everyone is perfect and sacred. No one is better or less than anyone else. Honoring body/mind wisdom is the key to defenselessness, while remembering that each body/mind is equal to all others. In Lemuria there was nothing to protect ourselves from, because life intended for us to learn, grow, and evolve. Thus, the need to defend one's self, ideas, or actions as they stemmed from the body/mind was unnecessary. Indeed, defensiveness only accomplished karmic repercussions, sometimes leading to the vicious circle of revenge. Furthermore, to be neutral, to not take sides, even in one's own issues, is the supreme defense.

We don't mean to roll over and play dead or to give up. We stood firm with our own body/mind wisdom. We could merely respond with "Thank you for sharing" or "I prefer not to." Defenselessness was giving up the need to explain, resist, contest, or apologize.

Giving and Receiving

Giving and receiving are part of the natural loop of Universal Laws. Paradoxically, when we receive, we are simultaneously giving. When we give, we also receive.

Giving can be in the form of tangible or nontangible gifts.

When we freely and lovingly give anything, especially non-tangible things, that "amount" goes into a universal bank account, in accordance with the Laws of Connection and Attraction. The Universe automatically withdraws from an individual's bank account, providing gifts to the owner of the account based on deposits. When one doesn't give, funds are over-drawn! When one gives frequently, the universal bank account grows and pays dividends.

A gift must be given freely and wholeheartedly. A gift given with the expectation of getting something in return is not a gift but a manipulation. A gift that later breeds resentment is not a gift at all, but is based on fear or guilt.

Receiving is just as important as giving, part of the "loop." To feel selfish, embarrassed, or guilty when receiving is to forget one's intrinsic worth. Not only that, but to be unable or unwilling to receive is an insult to the gift-giver. We found a simple "thank you" was sufficient.

Paradoxically, if one focuses primarily on receiving money or any other thing, then one is not involved in Universe Wisdom and generally experiences discontent and frustration. When we focused simply on giving and receiving, while intending to further our own and others' evolution and happiness, abundance flooded into our universal bank accounts as a result of the Laws of Connection and Attraction. To withhold or stop the flow of giving and receiving disrupts the abundant, natural flow of the universe, which can bankrupt one's universal bank account.

Respect

Since all manifestations of Creator Source are interconnected and eminently important, we respected and revered all humans, animals, plants, our planet, indeed all existence. Mother Earth is a living entity, with her own limitations and distinct processes of cleaning and nurturing herself, but she has been pushed beyond her natural cycles. For too long humankind has been disrespectful and arrogant, has forgotten the planet doesn't belong to us to do with as we wish. Because we are connected to her, when we hurt her, we hurt ourselves. She can and will regenerate herself if we respect her own innate wisdom. When we learn to live in harmony within Mother Earth's wisdom, she will regenerate, becoming unspoiled and abundant once again.

The same is true of human beings. When we respect our own and others' body/mind wisdom, inborn gifts, talents, and paths, we promote individual and global regeneration. As one is respectful, so one gains respect, the result of the Laws of Connection and Attraction.

Joyful Creation

Boredom is life without joyful, passionate creation. Passion is the juice at the core of creation. It's the molten lava that flows and shapes life in the cauldron of creation. Creation is an immutable part of the universe. Everything in the universe is undergoing constant creative evolution. Creativity is aligned with universal evolution.

Furthermore, creativity is a manifestation of one's soul including talents, desires, abilities, and characteristics. To avoid creativity is to ignore oneself and one's higher purpose in life. The path of creativity is right action when joy, happiness, and passionate excitement are experienced as a result. Whether the creation is a work of art or a more harmonious friendship, joy can be the guide. The universal bank account pays big dividends when one creates work that is playful, easy, and beloved. We knew in Lemuria that our life's work was intended to be joyful and we experienced abundance and pleasure from it.

Willingness

Willingness is a sign of true wisdom. To be willing to hear someone else, to be willing to learn something new, to be willing to grow, to be willing to make mistakes, to be willing to be as we are, to be willing to compromise, to be willing to honor body/mind wisdom—these are all steps to living the Lemurian Way. Willingness opens the heart. Often miracles happen simply by being willing. But willingness must never contradict body/mind wisdom. For example, to be willing to compromise when the body/mind says "no" is to create karmic repercussions and disharmony.

Empathy and Compassion

We couldn't judge another person because we weren't walking in another's skin, experiencing another's life. That lack of judgment we called compassion. If someone displayed anger or hate towards us, we knew there was some deep underlying unhappiness which we couldn't truly know, but we could feel empathy with the struggle, since all souls struggle at one point or another.

A lesson exists behind the struggle. The greater the struggle, the greater the lesson and the more profound the accomplishment when learned. We came to understand that learning has many levels and spirals, twists and turns on the road of life. But once a lesson is learned, it cannot be unlearned, and is permanent in the soul's record for all time. A soul absorbs the completion of its lessons as well as spiritual accomplishments and achievements within itself, into the spirit realm, and is broadcast throughout the entire universe. Empathy and compassion embody awareness of the struggle towards the Light and are two of the greatest lessons to be learned. Often, out of empathy and compassion comes unconditional love.

Unconditional Love, Alignment with Others, and Synchronicity

Unconditional Love

Since we are all connected, affecting and being affected by the universe, everyone who exists is important for overall evolution. Everyone holds an important piece of the universal jig-saw puzzle. To believe that one person is more or less important in the scheme of life is untrue. To recognize the value of all beings is unconditional love.

Some people confuse love with attachment and need, which can cause pain. When we didn't fulfill our own needs or believed we were incomplete, we experienced separation and conditional love. Conditional love feels heavy, produces resentment and a sense of being "imprisoned." Conditional love makes the object of our affection go away.

Nothing and no one belongs to us. All people and things exist for the benefit of all. Thus unconditional love has no conditions, expectations, or ownership. This kind of love is freedom for all involved and brings peace and harmony to relationships. Unconditional love is light and attracts people to us. One can unconditionally love a person, even if choosing not to be in that person's presence.

Alignment with others

Personal progress is connected to universal progress and benefits everyone.

Furthermore, as one moves forward on the path, one is aligned with those who are meant to assist in the learning process. Since we knew these important truths, we consciously and deliberately aligned with those who seemed to bring us the greatest joy as well as those who presented the greatest challenges, knowing that regardless of how our intellects saw individuals, everyone (and every lesson) was perfect.

Just like the universe, we grow and evolve within ourselves. As conscious spirits, we are constantly growing and evolving. Each time we learn, we expand and become wiser than we were before. Alignment contained a mysterious factor within it. As I transform myself, other people transform themselves in my presence." As we practiced various components of Universal Wisdom-like forgiveness, surrender, acceptance, or unconditional love—we transformed our individual selves. Because we are all connected, being in our transformed energy helped other people to transform themselves—*just by being around us.* Imagine that the Gold Light of Universal Wisdom is a virus, a beneficial virus, and highly contagious. This Gold Light virus is easily transmitted, just as a virus is spread from one person to the next, and just as quickly. We found we didn't even need to be in another's presence; the virus could be spread long distance.

The reason this virus works is because of the vast energy field that connects everything to everything. When one person vibrates in a new way, the entire energy field begins to shift and transform as well. Those closest to the new vibration feel it first, but it spreads rapidly. Can one person make a difference? Most definitely.

Synchronicity

Each person holds a piece of the universal jigsaw puzzle. Some people's pieces fit perfectly into our section of the puzzle and ours with theirs. We can sense this synchronicity when we encounter people we haven't met before. We instantly feel either an affinity or a repulsion for them, while others pass by without notice; their pieces not corresponding in any sense to our own. In Infinite Time, when certain pieces of the puzzle fit together, synchronistic events occur.

Mutual Support (Win/Win)

Everyone on Earth is essential to the overall growth of human consciousness, peace, harmony, and abundance. Each person holds a vital piece of the universal jigsaw puzzle. Therefore, the wisdom, desires, and goals of each of us is vital to everyone else. Unless everyone wins, no one wins. When keeping the win/win principle in mind, our negotiations became easy. Furthermore, when we supported and encouraged others in getting what they wanted, we opened the vault of the universal bank account—and all received abundance. Win/win also includes opinions and viewpoints. When we honored and respected others' opinions and viewpoints, everyone was a winner.

Conclusion

Threads of Universal Wisdom, like forgiveness or unconditional love, can be employed separately. But we found that when threads are practiced in unison (the whole cloth—all the pieces), grace grows exponentially. Furthermore, when two or more people merge via their conscious, unconscious, or super-conscious thoughts, this leads to a manifestation much greater than the sum of its parts, known as synergy. We knew this principle well, which is why we often worked in groups.

Of course, the form the manifestation will take is dependent on the type of thought utilized. If people are angry together, they manifest disharmony on a scale much larger than themselves. When people practice hate together, they create separation, disunity, even war. But when we used the threads of Universal Wisdom in positive synergy, such as forgiveness, surrender and unconditional love, and especially intention, we manifested grace, but far more immense and grand than merely the individual people involved. As we practiced different threads of Universal Wisdom as a group, grace became profound for all of us. Employing Universal Wisdom is easy. All that is required is practice.

Chapter Fifteen

Sacred Sites Today

We discovered an extremely easy way to practice Universal Wisdom and to align with Universal Law. We created our Gold Light Temples at sacred sites,.

Energy Grids and Energy Stations

As we discussed in Part I, we created our communities along energy grids. Our Light Temples were located on these energy grids, in vortices or energy stations. Each energy vortex had its own individual operation and purpose. These energy stations were powerful vibrational placements connected to Earth energy as well as linked to the cosmos. The Earth body, the physical body, and the universal body are aligned and united at energy vortices, bringing regeneration and strength to all. Vortices were also connected to Infinite Time.

Light Temples

Our Light Temples were configured using higher mathematics and a knowledge of higher dimensions and constructed on these energy vortices by Gold Light, thought, and intention. We then used group synergy to increase the vibrational impact of Light Temples and to further align them with Universal Laws, Universal Wisdom, and Creator Source. Crystals were included at Light Temples because of their ability to increase, transmit, and receive energy.

Consequently, our Light Temples were "schoolhouses" of the universe. We used them to learn and understand Universal Law and how to implement Universal Wisdom. We intuited our alignment with the universal jigsaw puzzle. Light Temples regenerated our physical bodies and sustained Mother Earth. Light Temples were connected to Infinite Time (or timelessness) and information of past and present "time" could thus filter through. Later in human evolution other civilizations created oracles at energy vortices, such as the one at Delphi. Messages could be transmitted even more powerfully at Light Temples, because of the vast energy oscillating there. Because Light Temples (at these energy vortices) were attached to many dimensions simultaneously, we could travel in our light bodies and communicate telepathically to other dimensions, galaxies, the spirit realm, as well as other Light Temples.

Sacred Sites Today

Lemurian knowledge was duplicated by many civilizations, particularly the Atlanteans (which was passed on to their colonies), especially during their retreat from their own submerging continent. Their sacred sites were created with esoteric Lemurian objectives in mind. Sacred sites around the world are a combination of many elements first known and practiced in Lemuria. This knowledge lasted for millennia, and all the sacred sites of today were created and positioned accordingly. The Pyramids of Egypt and Mexico, and other ancient sites such as Stonehenge, Avebury, Callanish Stone Circle, and countless others, are built using memories (similar to Rupert Sheldrake's theory of morphic fields) of the Earth's grids and energy centers, sacred geometry, along with the knowledge of how to create and activate their own sacred sites. The power of crystals and how to use them was also incorporated. Since they couldn't replicate energy in light the way we did, these subsequent civilizations put information in rock and stone. This information is available to any who visit these places by touching the stones and also using sound to open the corridors in the stone's vibrational body.

Thus, Lemurian know-how is in action to some degree at all sites today. Unfortunately, over many millennia, understanding of this mystical knowledge has been lost and is only recently is being rediscovered. Special locations exist where the geophysical environment can most easily enable individuals to experience altered states of consciousness. These include rocks with a high proportion of quartz crystal, zones where natural radioactivity is strong, or places which have specific magnetic peculiarities.

Circles and spirals were part of our sacred symbolism. These kinds of symbols are found in sacred sites around the world carved in stone, such as at Carnac in France, standing stones in Scotland, and the Mouraki boulders in New Zealand. We Lemurians also understood and utilized the vibrations of sun, moon, planets, stars, and galaxies and used this knowledge for creating our Light Temples. Robert Bauval has discovered that the complex of Pyramids in Giza are built in the pattern of Orion's belt, including Sirius and other stars. There are upward shafts leading diagonally from the King's and Queen's chambers, each of which is directed towards a specific star. Did the Egyptians believe they were creating a pathway for the King and Queen to "return home," much as we did when we traveled from our Light Temples to other galaxies? We Lemurians created longevity of our physical bodies utilizing our Light Temples, perhaps even appearing immortal to outsiders. Were Egyptian pyramids designed with Lemurian immortality in mind for pharaohs and their queens?

Consequently, sacred sites are both innately powerful as well as implanted with vibratory information intended to be passed on to all who visit. All sacred sites exist today with their vibrational impact unaltered, transforming, increasing, transmitting, and receiving energy and information. The impact of this is accumulative after visiting many sites.

There are numerous merits to visiting sacred sites which:

Activate cellular memories

Enhance soul memories and Universal Wisdom

Transform energy like a shower of energy and light

Activate psychic and intuitive abilities

Treat emotional, mental, and physical problems

Accelerate personal, group, and global evolution

Transform personal, group, and global karma

Regenerate, re-create, and revitalize the physical body, including DNA, the pineal gland and other glands

Connect with other sites and people around the globe, through the interlinking of energy grids and energy stations, creating oneness.

Visiting sacred sites enhances the Universal Law of Connection. Each site links up with other people who have been there and to other sacred sites. Sacred sites connect to the universe as a whole, to stars, planets, time, and other dimensions as well. Tour groups visit sacred sites today in ever-increasing numbers. The proprietors of many tour groups who exclusively visit sacred sites are spiritually-awakened souls who desire to bring others to sacred sites to experience the energy and wisdom there. They have studied mystical information on each site they visit, bringing the information to the participants. Sacred tour owners know the value of meditation and ritual, thus they provide many opportunities for participants to meditate and practice ancient rituals at these powerful sites.

Why travel with tour groups? Along with the knowledge that the tour group leaders possess, they understand the value of synergy, something which we Lemurians held dear. Synergy exponentially expands the energy and action of a site for the entire group of participants.

Why now? Many spiritual seekers sense an urgency, a desire to learn quickly. This is due to the acceleration of energy on the planet and the shift upwards in Earthly consciousness. Experiences at sacred sites can effect spiritual growth and healing in minutes that it might ordinarily take months or years to accomplish.

Sacred sites require energy to remain fully functioning instructional temples. When a sacred site is respected and honored, it further activates that site. To visit these places with respect, honor, and joy increases the output of energy and, through connection to Universal Wisdom, stimulates a desire for harmony with the Earth and Earth inhabitants.

Although famous sites like those mentioned above attract large groups of people, less famous ones also contain tremendous power. Each sacred site is situated on a different grid and/ or energy center. Therefore, the vibration is unique at each site, while affecting each person individually. Some sacred sites may be more powerful for one individual than another. Even though energy from a sacred site may not be apparent at the time, energy gets transmitted anyway. Often people experience transformational changes much later after a return home. Sacred sites are being lit up with increasingly intense waves of Gold Light. This is being done intentionally, to help the evolution of human consciousness on the planet. Gold Light, as we have mentioned before, is the light of transformation. Therefore, when participants visit sacred sites, they are being bombarded with the Light from Creator Source. Their lives, and the lives of all others they are attached to, are transforming as a result. They are learning Universal Laws and developing and enhancing their psychic and spiritual tendencies. In short, visiting sacred sites is healing individuals while transforming the planet.

Mental Sacred Sites

Mental sacred sites can activate energy and wisdom in much the same way as physical ones do. Archetypes, legends, myths, ideas, and stories in human memory banks contain the essence of our Lemurian lifestyle. Some of these are:

The Garden of Eden

Oz

Camelot

Wise man and wise woman

Santa Claus

Greek mythology

Goddess religions

Genesis

Indigenous myths

The Golden Age

Unconditional love

Soul mate & twin souls

Global village

Freedom

Universal brotherhood

All people are created equal

Divine child

Wise fool

Heaven

Home

 Nirvana

Even some Disney animated movies can be considered in this category, which may explain their universal appeal.

Creating Sacred Sites

One doesn't necessarily need to travel. Any place where Universal Wisdom is being practiced can become a sacred site. One's garden, home, office, or special meditative place can become a Light Temple. All that is needed is:

Earth (should be situated on the ground floor of a building; outside is even better)

A sacred water source (preferably running water such as a fountain or stream)

Intention to make the space sacred and holy

Invoking Gold Light

Group synergy to increase the vibrations (two or more people)

Sacred sound (like singing, chanting OM, or toning)

Crystals

Fire (candles)

Breathing in unison (especially in interconnected breaths; some yogic methods utilize this)

Practicing Universal Wisdom while at the sacred site (see previous chapter)

Personal sacred sites can be fun, illuminating, informative and may create some amazing, transforming experiences for those who use them.

Whatever way you choose to activate and enable Universal Wisdom into your life is valuable—you can change yourself and your world. Remember what the Elders say—one person can make a difference.

Chapter Sixteen

Conclusion

Now you can understand why we Lemurians were so meticulous and careful—bringing in specific souls, selecting the most appropriate mother and father for that soul, training our children's body/minds, creating Light Temples, connecting to the Gold Light, staying aligned with each other and Universal Wisdom—in all phases of our everyday life. Our goal was harmony and we left nothing to chance, but continued to practice and refine. As we exercised the entire complement of Universal Wisdom, we experienced grace, living within the Gold Light Canopy of harmonious attraction and connection. Our lives were easy, living in higher consciousness. But then we came to the end of our path.

What is your path? Many of you believe that a time is coming when the entire planet will shift into higher consciousness also known as ascension. But we tell you this shift has already happened. What many of you are now experiencing is expansion into this higher consciousness, learning to live harmoniously with each other in Universal Wisdom, based on Universal Laws. The space between spirit worlds and Earth has narrowed, the distance between them brought closer together. Ascended masters and spirit entities in other dimensions are helping you learn, while they are transmuting global karma, absorbing pain, protecting you and smoothing the way, so the Earth doesn't have to go through the painful metamorphosis of change alone. Angelic visitations are increasing. Gold Light is being beamed onto the planet in ever-increasing waves to individuals and groups, while the entire consciousness of planet Earth is growing in its warmth.

The future is mutable, based on alignment with this new higher consciousness. Some prophets have predicted that terrible cataclysms, catastrophes, and mass destruction will soon befall your beloved planet. This isn't predestined to happen, but is simply one avenue the future can travel. A second, and quite different, path requires a critical mass of Earth's inhabitants to access body/mind with the intention of living in harmony, peace, and unconditional love with each other and the planet; understanding Universal Law; and utilizing Universal Wisdom, which will lead to grace, the prophesied Golden Age. A harmonious gathering of energy could dramatically shift the planet's consciousness. This would prevent unnecessary suffering and further calamity from occurring. Many of you have been intuiting this for some time. We tell you it is real and possible. The vibration of the cosmos is ready to help you.

There are many other paths as well, encompassing some of each of these two opposite scenarios. Which path do you prefer? You hold a vital piece of the universal puzzle. The choice is yours.

Dear Gentle Spirits:
We have come to the end of our story. But you are beginning yours. All you have to do is remember and practice. It's easy. Our promise to you is that we will stay in touch with you always. We're available at any time, any place. Just call us and we'll be there. To dry your wings when they get wet. To nurture you and comfort you when you're cold and lonely. To whisper in your ear when you forget. To hold your hand as you walk towards understanding and Wisdom. And of course to applaud your achievements.
We'll always be waiting in the Gold Light.
We are the Elders and so are you.
With love and blessings forever —The Elders

Lauren's Afterthoughts:

Becoming an Elder

The energy and teachings of this book continue to deeply affect my life, as I'm sure the Elders intended. Perhaps *The Lemurian Way* will never be completely "finished," but will only continue to evolve.

Six months after the book was completed, I lost touch with the Elders. This was most distressing, since they've been more or less continuously in my life since I was five years old, teaching, nurturing, and encouraging me. I called them and called them but they didn't come into my consciousness. A week went by and I continued to try to make contact, but without success. Then one day after trying once more, I heard a tiny voice within my heart.

'What are you doing in there?" I asked with surprise.

"We've merged with you," they replied. "Now we are one with you!"

"But what will I do without you?" I inquired.

"You're an Elder-in-training now. Listen to yourself," they replied gently.

Consequently I have been practicing what the Elders so willingly and lovingly shared in this book. I don't have to be perfect. All I have to do is be willing to practice, learn, grow, and evolve. I feel honored that they trust me to carry the Lemurian torch. To be an Elder, as the book states, is to hold the energy of Lemuria, to carry Gold Light within me and embody Universal Wisdom. It's an important job, yet an easy and joyful one.

121

Furthermore, I realized that in order to "get into your most perfect and sacred work, first the work needs to get into you."

Lemurian Ceremony

I traveled to Hawaii in October, 1998, to visit a Lemurian sister/friend, Springs Romano, who performs ceremonies. We decided to do a ceremony that incorporated all the facets described in *The Lemurian Way*. The evening before the ceremony, I recognized that it was the first Lemurian ceremony performed in perhaps thousands and thousands of years. We held the ceremony at a sacred site (Olupu Heiau) on Oahu. The results were quite stunning. Together with the participants, we erected a Gold Light Pyramid, which many people could "see." Some saw glimpses of gold light shooting out from the altar. Were those Lemurians in spirit body? When doing the sacred becoming ritual, we could feel the Collective Heart of our group opening. During the ceremony several others and I were initiated as Elders-in-training. Since my initiation, I feel clearer, stronger, and more "solid" than I ever have been. I am honored to live this job.

In the days that followed, everyone who attended (both physically and telepathically) had life-enhancing experiences. Here's an example:

"Yesterday, I read your email about the First ever Lemurian Ceremony planned for Saturday night. As fate would have it, I was attuned a week ago to an advanced level of Reiki. Normally, one needs to adjust to the influx of new energies. I didn't think it would be a good idea to participate in this historic event. Around 9:30 P.M., I turned in, calling it a day. The next thing I knew, I was wide-awake and mentally alert. The vibrations in the room had changed. The reiki energy was coursing through my palms. With so much energy corning through, my hands were like Star Trek Phasers. "What's going on?" I thought, pondering the situation. A split second later, it hit me. "It's the Lemurian Ceremony in progress. I sat up in bed and tried to remember your email. Since I didn't want to spoil the moment by gathering the suggested items, I decided to touch my chakras as previously instructed. I didn't verbalize the statements because I would have needed a hard copy of your email to follow. No, I just touched my chakras, pausing in between to allow space for what was supposed to be my brief recitation ("Sacred Light" and so on). After completing all of my chakras (I'm not sure if I touched them all), I felt a heightened sense of awareness. This continued for an indefinite length of time. At some point I drifted off to sleep. Lemurian Elders, next time I'll be a willing participant. You won't have drag me along. Apparently, the Elders know who we are even if we don't!

Thank you Lauren. Thank you Lemurian Elders. Lauren when do you plan to do the next one? Maybe you could do it at Sedona, Arizona or at Ayers rock (Uluru) in Australia. Surely there must be fellow Lemurians in these areas?" —A Reiki practitioner

A week later I went to Burbank, California to lecture on Lemuria and hold another Lemurian ceremony. Again we all experienced the same sweet, loving energy. One attendee got to be initiated into her spiritual work. When I made the announcement, "You are now connected to your most perfect, sacred work," we both could feel a rush of energy into her crown chakra. This is powerful stuff! For the next thirty-six hours I experienced what I can only describe as a bliss state. Perhaps this is what it felt like to live in Lemuria. I was in love with the whole world and the rapture made me feel totally at peace, joyful, welcoming, and whole. In 1998, I visited Egypt and performed a Lemurian ceremony at the Temple of Hathor at Dendera.

Interesting information

Since finishing the book and becoming an Elder-in-training, I've had a number of revelations and visions that have greatly changed my outlook.

The first is the simple statement "Everything is perfect, no matter what it looks like, for the purpose of learning, growth and evolution." This means that everything happening in us and on our planet is meant for our growth, learning, and evolution. No longer do I think that there is bad stuff and good stuff happening. It's all just stuff. No matter what is going on, I just repeat to myself, "everything is perfect," and then I can see the perfection. It makes my life easy and full of fun.

The second turning point was a vision I received while having dinner with a friend. We were discussing President Clinton (this was before his Monica Lewinsky confession) and debating whether he was lying or telling the truth. Suddenly everything around me blacked out and all I saw were billions of swirling tornadoes of energy, which appeared as cornucopias. I discerned and was told that these cornucopia-tornadoes were each a separate universe that every soul inhabits within the larger universe. The information I received was that each separate universe is whole and complete unto itself, and, within that universe, all things are true. Each universe has its own truth, based on one's experiences, past lives, decisions, thoughts, beliefs, and so on. In that respect, there is no truth with a capital T, only many truths. And each person's truth is absolutely true and correct for that person. Therefore, whatever is true for someone is true. Period. For example, someone might have a broken window in his/her universe. And in someone else's universe, the window is not broken. And they are both true simultaneously! This means there is no reason for me to ever feel like I have the "right" answer while someone else is "wrong." We are both right. We simply live in separate universes.

The third revelation is that Earth was never meant to be a difficult place in which to live. It was originally intended to be a vacation spot for experiencing the third dimension, for having fun and experiencing the five senses and the loveliness of this world with all its inhabitants, flora, and fauna, and magnificent scenery. Earth was intended to be like Disneyland! (Mr. Toad's Wild Ride, anyone?)

The fourth is practicing gratitude—for everything, good, bad, and indifferent. I had spent many years being grateful for the good things but never for unpleasant experiences and feelings. This has been such a profound learning experience that I wrote an article on it, which I present below.

Gratitude

I'm a meta-scientist, which means that I'm always on the lookout for some new and improved way to live spiritually within the universe. One of the pieces of Universal Wisdom I have learned was gratitude, which I've practiced for many years. Whenever something wonderful, large or small, occurs I always remember to say "Thank you, God."

But then early this year I began to have an inkling that there was something more, a higher octave of gratitude. I needed to practice being grateful for the unpleasant things, too. I had already become aware that "everything is perfect" in the Universe, no matter what it looks like. Therefore, each lesson or challenge, regardless of its appearance, was a precious gift for my growth and evolution and linked to the Collective Consciousness as well. So I started to practice a new form of gratitude, being grateful even if the "negative something" never changed.

I had been sick with the flu for a week or two and decided it was a good place to begin. I began saying both out loud and in my head, "Thank you for this flu. I'm very grateful for being sick. I'm thankful that I can't get out of bed, have a fever, aches and pains, etc." At first it was only an exercise. Every time I said I was thankful, my conscious mind responded adversely.

"Are you crazy? How can you be grateful for this? It doesn't make any sense." But I doggedly persisted, ignoring my mind, feeling that somehow what I was doing was appropriate.

The first thing I noticed is that my mind slowly stopped protesting. A sense of peace and calm replaced my mind's antagonism. I didn't seem to care so much that I was sick in bed. In fact, I began to feel happy and content although I was still sick. "Hmmm," I thought. "This is interesting." I even encouraged my partner Paul Obler to practice, too. Instead of telling me how upset he was that I was sick, I asked him to say instead "I'm really thankful you're sick." I'm sure he thought I had lost a few of my marbles.

Then our car broke down and I continued to practice gratitude. "Oh, thank you so much for our car breaking down. I'm grateful we have to spend money to fix our car." And so on. Whatever unpleasant, unfortunate or upsetting event occurred, I countered with "I'm grateful," knowing that even if I didn't understand why the event was happening, it was somehow perfect. Calmness, peace, and happiness continued to grow each time I practiced.

I then began to look at other things. For example, I had put on quite a bit of weight in the last few years. I practiced being grateful for my weight. I practiced gratitude for money problems. In short, I started being grateful for everything I could think of. Serenity and joy continued to flood my conscious-ness. I found this shift to be quite fascinating and thought I was doing quite well with my newfound practice.

However, the Universe, in its wisdom, helped me deepen my understand-ing. On the fourth day of a three-month trip to Europe, I fell and badly sprained my right arm (I'm right-handed). Not only were we unable to travel because of the pain, but I also couldn't move my arm, couldn't dress myself, had difficulty feeding myself, even washing my hair. In short, I was severely hampered. So I practiced gratitude. Although I was somewhat bored sitting in a small Italian hotel room with only CNN for entertainment, I wasn't upset. I found that being grateful precluded anger, depression, and other unpleasant emotions. (Thank you for my boredom.) My arm healed rapidly, which is un-usual for me, and we began to travel again. Then when I returned home from my trip, I broke my toe. Immediately I was thankful for my broken toe and forgot all about it. In three days it had mended tremendously and in less than two weeks had completely healed.

I discerned that I had "stumbled" onto something powerful. Being grateful for what has been termed negative events means to fully embrace all of my life. In embracing all things in my life meant that I had moved from passive acceptance into active gratitude. In a sense, I was taking charge of my life and embracing responsibility for all things within it, which seemed to change my whole attitude towards negativity.

Then I turned my attention outward and began to practice gratitude for many things that exist on our planet such as pollution, war, hunger, violence, and so forth. My attitude toward those situations shifted dramatically as well. I'm not saying that I sit back and do nothing about negative situations. I do what I can and am led to do. However, in the meantime, I have a different and spiritual perspective on personal and world situations, which brings me much contentment and joy in my outlook and attitude.

People say they want peace and harmony in life. I've realized that peace and harmony are a state of mind, an attitude, rather than being linked to a pleasant event, situation, or condition. That state of mind can be achieved through grat-itude. Unfortunate, unpleasant, and inharmonious events and situations can and probably will continue to happen in life, but with gratitude the focus shifts from unhappiness and despair to serenity, harmony, and happiness.

"Thank you, God."

Lauren O. Thyme

Scientists and the Lemurian Way

Sometimes during the writing of *The Lemurian Way*, I wondered how the information within this book squared with scientific thought. Since finishing and publishing this book, I have had synchronistic experiences that have shed some scientific light on *The Lemurian Way*. The first experience happened when my partner Paul brought home a copy of *Life* magazine for me, because it had an article on astrology in it. Within the article was a brief discourse on David Bohm, a physicist and protégé of Einstein's. According to the article,* Bohm (like many other physicists) had been disturbed that an electron could be both a wave and a particle. After twenty years of talking to spiritual masters like Krishnamurti and the Dalai Lama, Bohm came up with a concept that "…linked theorems like the Schrodinger equation to the insights of mystics. The Universe, Bohm proposed, is a holo-movement, a single unbroken entity in flowing motion." I was very excited. This was a restatement of the single Universal Law the Elders had discussed: "Everything is connected to everything."

Later I tuned into a program on *The Learning Channel* featuring Rupert Sheldrake, a foremost biologist. Sheldrake, through years of observation and experimentation, had come up with a theory about morph fields. Although I can't claim to understand his theory fully, I gathered that a morph field both surrounds each of us and is also linked to everything else. Thus, if one individual or group of people (or birds or animals) learn something, the learning goes out into the morph field and others can learn it by a form of osmosis. This time, though, the learning is easier. Again, everything is connected to everything.

129

I had read some of Carl Jung's writings many years ago. Paul pointed out that Jung's theory of collective consciousness is similar to the idea that "everything is connected to everything." Paul is an eclectic scientist and enjoys reading broadly and amassing information from many sources. He told me that much of much of what we wrote in this book has been theorized and expounded on by many others—not only by Jung, but also by William Blake, William Butler Yeats, John-Paul Sartre, and Wilhelm Reich, to name just a few.

Neither Sareya nor I had read any of the works written by these people, and I found it amazing that we had gathered these diverse theories into our one small volume. Morph fields, collective consciousness, the holo-movement and Universal Law (as stated by the Elders) all seem to indicate an intact, connected, and flowing tapestry of awareness.

Lastly, a dear friend of mine, Phil Stone, an engineer, architect, and draftsperson, told me that *The Lemurian Way* appeared to restate Einstein's theory of relativity. I cannot comment on that since I have never read or studied Einstein. However, again I found the information quite interesting.

Over the last few years, I noticed that many people are going through transformational experiences. I watched my daughter, dear friends, and others struggle with this development. One day information jumped into my awareness and I wrote it down. The article has begun to travel around the world via the Internet and other people's newsletters. Please feel free to share it.

Cracking the Cosmic Egg

A global development of immense proportions is transpiring on our beloved planet. Time as we know it is mutating, speeding up, accelerating, and expanding. Energy and vibration is increasing and heightening, changing our molecular structure and DNA, moving us forward, pushing us past our old limitations, and shifting us into a new awareness. Two events helped to stimulate this process or were perhaps aligned with it. One was the Harmonic Convergence in the 1980s, the other the conjunction of Uranus and Neptune in 1993. Coupled with these, we're experiencing more concentrated solar flares and a destruction of our ozone layer; we are thus being bombarded by vast universal forces. Furthermore, nonphysical beings from other dimensions and realms, angels, and ascended masters are sending guidance, Gold Light, and Love to assist our global shift. Walk-ins who've come to serve are arriving in ever-greater numbers, consisting of both "new souls" and "future selves." In addition, highly spiritual Lemurian energy from both incarnate and discarnate souls is more intensely entering our group consciousness. The cosmic orchestra is tuning up.

Many individuals worldwide are experiencing vast, abrupt, and unexpected shifts of consciousness and an acceleration of perception as the veil of spiritual forgetfulness is removed—a "cracking of the cosmic egg." This has led to transformation and alterations in the physical, emotional, and psychological as well as one's spiritual body.

Although the shift is a positive one and will eventually usher in peace, harmony, unity, and other joyful states of being, some side effects may be experienced. These can be difficult, even painful, but they are only our physical, psychological, and mental bodies trying to accommodate to massive changes.

Unpleasant physical sensations can range from dizziness, disorientation, ringing or buzzing in the ears, weight loss or gain, nausea, vomiting, feeling a vague sense of illness, unaccustomed fatigue or overwhelming desire to sleep, insomnia, headaches (especially in the third eye region), unusual aches and pains, and a (sometimes painful) heightening of the five senses of smell, vision, hearing, touch, and taste. Strange "light shows" can play before one's eyes in darkness or before going to sleep. Psychological sensations can include difficulty coping with relationships that had been heretofore easy and normal with friends, family, home, or work environment. One can experience new problems functioning and a general impression of being "out of it." A disquieting sensation that everything in one's life, especially one's own self, feels new and different may permeate one's awareness. The old self may appear to be sloughing off; visions or dreams of stepping out of the old self can take place. Some individuals may literally "wake up" in the morning to this unaccustomed newness.

Sudden episodes of confusion, anxiety, fears, crying, or turbulent emotions can course through the psychological body, leaving one overwhelmed. Strange dreams can disturb sleep. In the waking state one can feel as though an altered state is occurring without benefit of meditation.

Disturbing sensations don't always accompany the awakening process, or they may be much milder than described above. Generally, all discomforting side effects will disappear, although they may sometimes linger for weeks or months. This "cracking of the cosmic egg" can be blamed on a virus, stress, or anyone of a hundred excuses. However, the rupture, accompanied by a distinct feeling of metamorphosis, is unmistakable.

On the other hand, transformational changes can be agreeable and gentle, pleasant and blissful. One ultimately becomes emotionally, psychologically and spiritually stronger and clearer. Challenges are handled in new and better ways, with a wiser and more insightful attitude. Difficult relationships either end suddenly and painlessly, or an improved relationship emerges miraculously from the rubble.

A new relationship with self also surfaces along with a heightened awareness of body/mind intuition, knowing, and wisdom.

This radical personal development is meant to shift the old paradigm from fear to forgiveness, unconditional love, detachment, surrender, mutual support, intention, defenselessness, and many other aspects of Universal Wisdom. "Cracking one's cosmic egg" is a good thing and necessary in order to bring a higher vibration of consciousness: to heal one's self, others, and Mother Earth, and to acquire a sense of oneness and unity. An individual's transmutation moves all of us towards a state of grace, since we are all connected. The generations who are now alive on the planet are the seed pods for global transformation, germinating, sprouting, and maturing into full aliveness and spiritual recognition. As more people experience this awakening, emerging from the egg of diminished consciousness, they are able to help others do the same. However, the process is as easy as spreading the flu, a positive kind of flu, one that most people would like to catch. The transformation virus is highly contagious. Others may catch this flu virus in our presence, who may then awaken, shift, and transform in front of our eyes. Celebration time is at hand. We're readying ourselves for a redistribution of leadership, the dismantling of power and control over others, and the beginning of full cooperation, unity, mutual support, and harmonious interaction. No longer do we need to think in terms of "them" and "us"—only us. We can cease to adhere only to our families, our tribes, our countries, and enfold the world village to our bosoms, into our hearts, and into our lives. Karma is coming to an end on our planet to be replaced with joy and living in grace. We are emerging from our narrow egg of awareness into the Light of a brilliant new day.

——Lauren O. Thyme, published in *HeartLinks* & *The Isis Connection, 1999*

A Lemurian Playground

After several years of playing with the concepts of Universal Wisdom and learning to both listen to and confer with my body/mind, I felt like I was ready for more. I wanted to become a Lemurian, with all those life-enhancing concepts as second nature to me. I wanted playmates who also wanted to grow and evolve with those same principles. I found Andrew Lutts, Salem New Age Center at *www.lemuria.net* and got those playmates.

Was Lemuria a real place in the dim mists of time? Or did I tap into a collective desire for *The Lemurian Way* to be real? Is Lemuria being created or re-created? I don't know with certainty, and frankly it doesn't matter to me anymore. All I know and believe is that it is possible and attainable for each of us, all of us, to create an edenic existence here and now, living the Lemurian Way, on this beautiful, blue-green planet, third from the sun.

Who are Lauren O. Thyme and Sareya Orion?

We have both been highly psychic since early childhood. We remember many past lives, including the one we lived in Lemuria. Individually we've heard the Elders' voices for many years, helping us to grow and learn, using our talents for psychic and spiritual counseling, healing, and nurturing. Several years ago we were brought together to become friends and to subsequently write this book. We knew the Elders through our clairvoyant, clairaudient, and clairsentient abilities and wrote down their transmissions. Thus, we are simply the messengers, although we feel highly honored the Elders chose to relate their message through us. This book wrote (or re-wrote) us. Lemurian knowledge, wisdom, and compassion has become a great gift in our lives. Our collaborative effort brought us tremendous insight into the simplicity and harmony of the universe and changed the way we see the world. We were taught the Lemurian Way and initiated into Lemurian rituals. We laughed and cried and learned together, often writing from morning until after midnight. We lived, ate, and breathed this book, as did the Lemurians when performing their work. We clearly hear and feel the Elders' passion—to stimulate the heart of the world and to remind us of our collective essential spiritual nature. We believe their affectionate nature will embrace you as you read *The Lemurian Way: Remembering Your Essential Nature.*

With Gold Light blessings always—

Lauren O. Thyme is a spiritual and psychic counselor, channel, medium, healer, visionary, professional astrologer, author and spiritual pilgrim.

 **Sareya Orion** is a natural healer and psychic and runs her own bodywork business using those talents. She is a true Lemurian artist, with a love of and training in beautiful décor, clothing, and personal adornment.

Facebook: https://www.facebook.com/lauren.thyme
https://www.facebook.com/sareya.sareya
Email: thyme.lauren@gmail.com
Websites: https://thymelauren.wixsite.com/thymely-one
www.LaurenOThymecreations.com

Books in print and ebooks at Amazon.com (under Lauren O. Thyme)

Other Books on Lemuria

Cerve, Wishar S. *Lemuria: The Lost Continent of the Pacific.* January 1931.

Childress, David Hatcher. *Lost Cities of Ancient Lemuria & the Pacific.* Adventures Unlimited Press, 1988.

Churchward, Col. James. *The Lost Continent of Mu.* Brotherhood of Life, 1992.

Churchward, Col. James. *The Children of Mu.* Brotherhood of Life, 1992.

Churchward, Col. James. *The Sacred Symbols of Mu.* Brotherhood of Life, 1996.

Churchward, Col. James. *Cosmic Forces of Mu*, Vol. 1 & Vol. 2. Brotherhood of Life, 1992.

Churchward, Col. James. *The Books of the Golden Age: The Sacred & Inspired Writings of Mu.* Brotherhood of Life, 1997.

Dennerline, Jerry. "Qian Mu and the World of Seven Mansions." Asian Studies

Earl of Ronaldshay. *Lands of the Thunderbolt: Sikhim, Chumbi, and Bhutan.* 1987.

Essene, Virginia, and Sheldon Nidle. *You Are Becoming a Galactic Human.* 1995.

Hayes, Christine. *Red Tree: Insight Into Lost Continents, Mu, and Atlantis.*

Highben, Denny. *Three Worlds Lost: The History of Mu, Lemuria, & Atlantis.*

Jungclaus, David. *Lemurian Atlantean Vision Wheel.* August 1991.

Kimpton, Roberta Rhodes, and Robert Walker (illustrator). *Lemuria: Soul Mates.*

Klein, Bette. Mylhi: *A Novel of Temple Life in Lemuria.* 1997.

Kueshana, Eklal. *The Ultimate Frontier.* The Adelphi Organization, 1991.

Lailel, Telos. *Messages From Adama.* Box 10945, Rochester, New York 14610-3041. LAILEL@aol.com.

Lazaris. Discover the Dreamer From Lemuria. Audiocassette, 1991.

Lazaris Remembers Lemuria. Audiocassette. Steven Boone, 1987.

Lazaris Remembers Lemuria. CD, Steven Boone, 1985.

Manley, David L. *Aros of Atlantis.*

Ni, Hua Ching. *The Mystical Universal Mother: The Teachings of the Mother of Yellow Altar*. 1991.

Norman, Ruth. *Lemuria Rising* Vall. Paperback, January 1976.

Norman, Ruth. *Lemuria Rising* Vol 2. Paperback, January 1976.

Norman, Ruth. *Lemuria Rising* Vol. 4. Paperback, January 1976.

Norman, Ruth. *Ra-Mu of Lemuria Speaks*. 1988.

Quan Yin, Amorah. *The Pleiadian Perspective*. Bear & Company, 1995.

Rigopoulo, Antonio. Dattatreya-*The Immortal Guru, Yogi and Avatara: A Study of the Transformative and Inclusive Character of a Mu*. 1998.

Rose, Delfina. *Star Song Oracle*. Hampton Roads Publishing, 1997.

Scott-Elliot, W. *Legends of Atlantis and Lost Lemuria*. Quest Books, Wheaton, Illinois, 1990.

Scott-Elliot, W. *The Lost Lemuria*. 1904; 1997.

Shafer, Gloria. Origins of the Children's Song Cycle as a Musical Genre with Four Case Studies and an Original Cycle (Studies in the History and Interpretation of Mu). 1989.

Spence, Lewis. *Problem of Lemuria: The Sunken Continent of the Pacific*.

Stein, Diane. *Dreaming the Past, Dreaming the Future*. Crossing Press, 1991.

Steiner, Rudolf. *Cosmic Memory: Atlantis and Lemuria*. 1981.

Symonds, N., et al. *Phage Mu*. 1987.

Zetland, Lawrence John, and Lumley Dundas. *Lands of the Thunderbolt: Sikhim, Chumbi, & Bhutan*.

Lemurian Websites

www.lemuria.net

www.powersthatbe.com/pstkalua.htm

www.thule.org/lemuria.html

www.crystalinks.com/lemuria.html

e-mail: springs@powersthatbe.com Springs Romano

To order additional copies of this book, please send full amount for each book plus $4.95 for postage and handling for the first book and $2.00 for each additional book to:

Lauren O. Thyme Publishing
1500 Pacheco St, #104
Santa Fe, NM 87505
Thyme.lauren@gmail.com

Specify if you wish to have copy autographed and to what name.

Or you can order print copies or ebooks from Amazon.com

.

Printed in Great Britain
by Amazon